P1

"A *Place at* ι reminds us that grace abounds even in the most desolate of circumstances. Katherine's spiritual journey is a triumphant one. Her story is full of encouragement for all of us on the spiritual journey."
—Susan Delaney, MD, MS

"Katherine DeGrow has penned an eloquent testimony to the strength of the human spirit. *A Place at the Table* is a touching and eloquent autobiography. The book looks back at the life of a young girl navigating through the changing values of the 20th century, from European immigrant customs in the early decades, to the WWII culture in the United States, to modern decades.

The story deals with the challenges women (and men) faced with their cultures and the role of women in a rapidly evolving society. Katherine navigated through the biases and customs of family, religion, gender inequality, and more.

Through it all, Katherine's strong values and growing self-awareness, as well as her keen observations of life around her and her determination to succeed make for a fascinating read. In the end it is her faith, and her thirst for an ultimate truth about God and man, enabled her to survive and thrive."
—Bob Schwaller, Christian Science Practitioner

"Katherine takes readers on a candid journey into her turbulent childhood and many difficult defining moments that follow. *A Place at the Table* is a powerful, personal, passionate recounting of the author's brave struggle to never again succumb to the demons of depression. Helpful, hopeful and empowering, her survival story affirms that no matter what others have done, no matter how dark the past and how great the pain, there can be love, grace, redemption and new dreams. A must-read and a must-share."

—Annette Bridges, Author of *The Gospel According to Momma* and other inspirational books for women and children

A PLACE at the TABLE

A Memoir

KATHERINE DEGROW

To Susan with
great appreciation
Katherine

A Place at the Table

A Memoir

Katherine DeGrow

The events in this book are true. The author has tried to recreate events, locales and conversations from her memories of them and has documented these to the best of her ability.

The author of this book does not dispense medical advice or prescribe the use of any technique as a form of treatment for physical or medical problems. The intent of the author is only to offer information about her life which may help you in your quest for emotional and spiritual well-being. In the event you use any of the information in this book for yourself, which is your constitutional right, the author assumes no responsibility for your actions.

All Biblical references in this book are derived from
The New Jerusalem Bible.

Library of Congress Cataloging-in-Publication Data

DeGrow, Katherine
A Place at the Table: A Memoir / Katherine DeGrow
2014921388

ISBN: 1502871181
ISBN-13: 978-1502871183

To Amy,
a precious daughter
who will ever remain in my heart.

"All which thy child's mistake
Fancies as lost, I have stored for thee at home:
Rise, clasp My hand, and come."

—Francis Thompson
"The Hound of Heaven"

CONTENTS

Dedication

Part I

Part II

Part III

Part IV

PART I

CHAPTER 1

STRUCK ON CHAMBLEE ROAD

The ancient Hebrews knew the importance of remembering. Going back in thought and in their worship, they recalled what God had done for them in the past, calling them out of slavery and into the vast desert wilderness and a long journey to the Promised Land. We, too, are called to remember, especially in times of darkness and fear. When we no longer feel at home or know the way, it is time to remember.

One Monday afternoon in the spring of 1973, driving my Volkswagen Beetle on Chamblee Road in suburban Atlanta, I was struck, not by another motorist but by Grace.

The spring day had not started well and after getting the kids off to school, I crawled back in my bed and tried to sleep in an attempt to escape the turmoil in my head. My mind would not stop its endless stream of noise—

fragments of thoughts soaked in feelings of confusion and intense loneliness.

My husband Doug and I had spent the weekend at a retreat called Religious Studies put on by the Ecumenical Institute based in Chicago. A new friend, Sandy, had attended one of their weekend retreats and urged me to go after she heard of my dilemma with the church: burned out from work and finding no inspiration in worship or anything I was doing for the cause of the Christian way, I'd had enough.

In my estimation, the weekend was horrific. At the last minute, it was necessary to move the meeting place from a retreat center to an Episcopal church where there were cots for sleeping but no showers for keeping fresh. Spending the night in the same space with twenty or so people, snorers and gas-passers, did not suit me in the least. To make matters worse the promised good food was replaced with mediocre sandwiches or tasteless noodle concoctions.

The curriculum was another thing altogether with papers by Bonhoeffer, Neiburh, Bultman, and Tillich. It felt like religious brainwashing, and I resisted full participation every inch of the way. Truth was I understood little that I read or heard. Now, that Monday morning after found me unable to get rid of the theological gibberish in the papers and lectures. I felt miserable.

Sleep continued to escape my grasp, but I kept fulfilling a definition of insanity attributed to Einstein,

"Doing the same thing over and over again and expecting a different outcome. Two phone calls interrupted my dis-ease that morning, the first from my friend Sandy who had urged us to attend the weekend event.

"I thought I would have heard from you by now," she said.

"I don't want to talk now. It was worse than awful." The conversation came to a quick end. Climbing back into bed, giving my pillow a good punch, I tried again to escape through sleep.

At about 2 p.m., the second call came in. It was my neighbor Jeanne. Could I possibly go to Chamblee High to pick up her son? "I've had an accident," she said. "Nothing major, no one hurt, but I have to wait for the police, and John is expecting me to pick him up."

"Yes, I can do that," I replied. My willingness to do something for another person might well have been a pivotal decision in light of what was to come.

Pulling on an old warm-up suit, I made my way downstairs and into the garage where my red Beetle awaited me. After backing out of our steep Atlanta driveway, hoping the after school traffic had not yet commenced, I headed toward Chamblee Road. Shifting into first gear after the stop sign and moving onto Chamblee, my eyes caught sight of a profusion of deep blue in the front of Miss Lily Bolton's house. The iris had fully opened over the weekend. The pause and sense of delight at seeing them made room for the fresh thought that slipped into my weary brain. "If sense could be made of just one thing from the weekend, perhaps I could stop the mental struggling and find some peace. What might that one thing be?"

Let's see. There was a sermon by Paul Tillich that had caught my attention for a bit. What was it about? Ah yes, its title was *You Are Accepted,* and included a definition of sin and grace. *What did it say again*? It came to me— *sin was defined as separation.* Before it is an act, it is separation from oneself, from others and from what Tillich called "The Ground of Being," his name for God. Even though I had avoided the sins preached about from the pulpits over the years—stealing, bearing false witness, coveting—I had never before heard sin defined as separation. *OK, I get it.* Sin is separation from myself, separation from others and, since I could feel no connection whatsoever to God, I would have to say I am a sinner. Hmm.

What about grace? What did Tillich have to say about this illusive term? Grace is just accepting the fact that you are accepted by that which is eternal, the One Creator, God. Grace is accepting that I am accepted.

After speaking the definitions aloud several times, I was struck! Something happened in the 'wink of an eye' that to this day defies adequate description. A brilliant yet gentle light entered the top of my head, streamed down the center of my body and into the car's floorboard, the brilliance unequal to any I'd ever witnessed. Then the words, *"That's it.* Nothing more and nothing more was needed. "That's it." The car now ablaze with holy light and me lifted to a place of peace and love I had never felt before, I was dumbstruck, amazed, filled with awe.

Continuing on Chamblee Road, I wondered if the glow was apparent to other motorists. *Should I say something to John about it when I picked him up? Would words come out of my mouth? Would he perceive the light and ask what was going on?*

John spotted me as I took my place in the line of cars forming in front of Chamblee High. Sprinting toward me, opening the passenger side and settling in, he told me his mom had called the office to let him know I was picking him up. If he noticed anything unusual about the atmosphere in the little vehicle he said nothing about it.

His boyhood vocals had recently been transformed into a mellow bass quality, quite pleasing to the ear. Odd I hadn't noticed before. After all, he did spend a good bit of time at our house because of his friendship with our son, Rusty.

John exited the car at the end of our driveway to walk the few houses to his own, leaving me to ponder my experience on Chamblee Road. I would have some time to do just that before my own lively kids came through the back door.

CHAPTER 2

WHAT NEXT?

It soon became clear that the experience on Chamblee Road was the beginning of something brand new—not just a break in the depression that had been my "off and on" companion for so many years. What I couldn't know then was that a long and difficult journey stretched before me. Within a matter of weeks the euphoria wore off and the questions began.

There was no doubt in my mind that it had been an experience of *God* or *Ground of Being* or just plain *Being,* never mind the title. The time had come to examine some of the ideas I had taken in as a child. I had long ago given up the notion of an old man sporting a white beard, sitting on a throne way above us, watching in order to punish us humans for our mistakes. Now I wanted to delve deeply into the mystery that had struck me with Grace on Chamblee Road. Our minister suggested the book, *The Life of Teresa of Jesus, The Autobiography of St. Teresa of Avila.* Her life story described spiritual experiences and, as she called them, the favors which the Lord had granted her as well as the spiritual trials she endured. Written at another time in terms unfamiliar to me, I looked for other authors who might give me understanding. Coming upon William James's *Variety of Religious Experience*, I struggled to digest his philosophy, yet I yearned to know more.

Despite my fears about caring for home, husband and three off springs, and asking myself if I could do it all, in the fall of that year I enrolled in Mercer University, Atlanta for courses in Religion and Psychology. There was no thought of getting a degree; I only wanted more understanding and direction for the future. What a trip it turned out to be. At times juggling demands of family and study was so hard I might have decided against it had I known beforehand. As it turned out the adventure was so exhilarating I was often left in awe. For one thing, I rediscovered my love of learning.

The nation was in the throes of great change as the women's movement followed on the heels of the Civil Rights era. Relationships were developing with other budding feminists who were returning students and a sense of excitement filled my days. It was a time of recovery—of excavating much that had been hidden in me. The religion classes led me to an examination of beliefs that had become fodder for depression. Imagine church teachings doing this. C. S. Lewis became a favorite author. In the preface of *The Great Divorce*, he wrote, "A sum can be put right: but only by going back till you find the error and working it afresh from that point, never by simply going on. Time does not heal it. The spell must be unwound, bit by bit."

My life was changing and the road before me beckoned. The fear of depression returning in the way it had disabled me as a teenager did surface periodically. *Was it a thing of the past or should I expect it to rear its ugly head again? What if I had to be hospitalized again?* There were times when subtle invitations to go into the darkness came but nothing like what I had experienced in the past. I learned that regular exercise and identifying the occasional low feelings and writing about them, kept me moving in the right direction.

I jumped into my courses with both feet relishing the challenge and new sense of confidence at being back in school. Toward the end of the second year my new faculty adviser said I was well on the way to a double major in religion and psychology. Why didn't I declare my intentions to graduate? I decided to go for it!

I also decided to apply for a Local Preacher's License offered by my denomination, the United Methodist Church. I had heard of one woman in the Atlanta area who had the License and thought it would be a good thing to do even though I didn't expect to preach. I pictured myself giving a talk or teaching. Obtaining this license required three things: a course of self-study, being questioned by a board as to my fitness to preach, and a sponsoring church. After talking to our minister who had become a friend of our family, I officially asked the congregation for their endorsement. I received it despite a number who did not raise their hands to be counted when the vote was taken.

After the vote was taken a man who was on the board of the church approached me with a question.

"Haven't you ever read Paul's words that a woman should not teach men and is to keep silent in the church?" (1 Corinthians 14:34)

Having recently completed a course on Paul's writings at Mercer, I responded that I was aware of it. "There are many such rules in Paul's writings and in other books of the Bible that are not practiced today. What of passages that direct slaves to be obedient to their masters?" (Ephesians 6:5)

A moment of silence and then he turned to join his wife who was standing nearby. It would be the first of many confrontations to come.

A month later I sat before the committee overseeing the Local Preacher's License. Was I nervous? Yes, decidedly so. In fact I wondered why I had started the process by declaring my intentions. I might never use the License if no one wanted me to speak to a congregation. Still there might be an Adult Sunday School class that would want a speaker and the study itself would surely be helpful to me. I sat primly on the blue padded chair across from the six clergymen on the committee. There were no windows to look out at the sunshine, only walls with a number of framed degrees and pictures of former pastors who had served that particular church.

It was a short interview with a few questions about my history in the local church and my classes at Mercer. The chairman of the group then asked the question "What does your husband think of all this?" I responded that he was totally supportive.

I came prepared to tell them about the experience on Chamblee Road. *Maybe another time,* I thought. I was glad when the meeting ended.

Graduation day at Mercer and the honor of graduating Summa Cum Laude came while preparing for a move to Dallas, Texas where Doug had been transferred by his company. After the move and a year of settling into a new home and getting kids in their respective schools, I was ready to enter seminary at Southern Methodist University, Perkins School of Theology.

CHAPTER 3

SEMINARY: MORE THAN
I BARGAINED FOR

Depressive feelings continued to nibble away at my enthusiasm throughout my first year at Perkins. It had been more than four years since my experience of Grace on Chamblee Road, and now I wondered if I would be dragged into darkness again. The question sent me looking for a therapist, a search made easy when a woman on the Perkins faculty told me of a psychologist who was highly regarded in the community. She was a consultant for the intern program for third-year students. I made an appointment with Dr. Gladys Brown.

Walking into her office, anxious over beginning what I sensed would be a daunting task; I was comforted by the garden-like open space in full view outside a wall of windows. Shadows played through the Live Oak trees cutting the glare of the Texas sun. After a few words of introduction she indicated with a slight flourish of her hand that I could sit in a leather chair across from her own. I guessed her age to be around sixty but I wouldn't swear by it. She was about my height, five feet five or six, had short graying hair and a rich Southern accent. She picked up a clipboard and pen lying on her chair, sat down and we began what would be many months of hard work.

At about the same time, a group of graduate students came together calling themselves simply, Perkins Women. I became a member and soon found it moving me in the same direction as my therapy was taking me. The Women's Movement sweeping through the country in the 1970s added to my strong resolve to stay the course.

In short order the dean took note of our plans to hold a Women's Week Symposium and commented that the women students were "running in packs." Several women laughed at his analysis but I admitted to myself that I was angry over it. About that time I discovered through my work with Dr. Brown that depression was covering past anger as well as anger that arose in the present.

Oh God, not anger! I was so uncomfortable with the emotion. Yet, as the weeks and months commenced, there was no denying it. Having had no role models in handling what, *nice girls should not feel,* I did everything from diluting my rising fury with tears to acting like a wild woman, going on tirades over injustice, including injustice tolerated and perpetuated by the church based on Biblical interpretation.

Many years later I would find an explanation for what occurred during those seminary days when reading the books of Eckhart Tolle. In *A New Earth* he describes anger from the past that has become trapped in consciousness and is periodically triggered to become active again. Anger and pain in the present is added to it. His term for this negative energy is *the pain body.* Based on this definition I would say mine became activated as I studied the history of the patriarchal church, the attitudes toward women by those who led the church, as well as the lies women had come to believe about themselves.

The energy was not only uncomfortable but unpredictable. Filling journal after journal as Dr. Brown urged me to do; I showed up at her office each week to spew out more of my anger and pain. She didn't flinch. She stayed with me, encouraged me to put words on the torrent of feelings I had not known were buried deep within me.

"You are clearing out old stuff and are finding out who you truly are in the process" she told me.

"Well, what if I go through all this to 'find my true self' and just find emptiness or someone I don't like?" I responded.

"You will like who you find," she answered matter-of-factly.

I kept going.

Along with Dr. Brown's compassionate and strong help, Perkins Women came to the rescue in the fall of my second year when our group invited Dr. Mary Daly from Boston College to be the keynote speaker for Women's Week. Dr. Daly's theme was the Exodus and the long, hard journey the Hebrew people faced on their way to the Promised Land. While in the wilderness many lamented leaving Egypt. At least they had enough to eat there. Had Moses brought them out to this forsaken land to let them die? (Exodus 16:3) Wanting to go back to old ways that seemed easier was women's sin. It was not pride, as we had been taught, but rather pure and simple sloth. And what was sloth, after all, but laziness, inertia, sluggishness. I got it and felt a determination to carry on, facing whatever issues might come up, working hard, and going where I could best determine God was leading me.

CHAPTER 4

LOST IN TRANSLATION

I began to wonder what effect some of the stories about women in the Bible might have had on me as a child, that is if I had heard them. I was coming across them in reading assignments and in books by feminist theologians. In the Moses story there were midwives who went about saving male children after a command from Pharaoh that they all be killed at birth. The Hebrews were growing in numbers and beginning to be seen as a threat to the Egyptians.

Shiphrah and Puah, are portrayed as courageous women (Exodus 1:5) standing up to Pharaoh because of their allegiance to God. They were named whereas many in scripture are simply referred to as someone's wife or daughter with their status found through their fathers or husbands. It struck me as odd that I had not noticed these two women in my reading of the Exodus story in the past. I did, however, recall Miriam, Moses's sister, who played an important part in the drama. She followed her mother's orders to go to the river to watch over Moses when he had grown too big to be hidden from Pharaoh's executioner. When he was discovered there by Pharaoh's daughter, Miriam told her she knew of a woman who could nurse and care for him. Moses is seen as having his own mother to raise him. This same sister played a tambourine, sang and danced after the Israelites successfully crossed the Sea of Reeds. I would have loved that story as a child. She had courage and celebrated with music and dance.

During the time of the Judges, thirteen centuries before Jesus birth, Deborah became a heroine who led her people against a king of Canaan, Jabin, who oppressed Israel by destroying vineyards and killing her people. Her importance did not end there. In her role as judge she became a counselor known for sitting under a date palm tree in front of her house giving counsel to those who came to her. I'm sure I would have been happy to know about Judge Deborah as a child. She too expressed courage along with wisdom.

In the New Testament I discovered a woman who lived in the temple compound. (Luke 2:36-38) She was 84 years old and spent her days serving God, fasting and praying. When she saw Mary and Joseph with their infant son, Jesus, she praised God and declared the babe to be the one who would deliver Israel. I had heard of Simeon, Anna's male counterpart, but never her. I began to wonder what was going on. Women were included in many places of scripture but their stories may not have been seen as important enough to teach or preach about, at least not in the churches I attended.

The first book I found on the subject of women and Christianity, *All We Were Meant to Be* by Letha Scanzoni and Nancy Hardesty, left me with amazement and joy. It also shocked me. In one place a quote is included on the purification rites women went through after giving birth. If a daughter was born the time involved was double that for a boy. "(The ritual) teaches us that not only has the curse thus fallen on the woman, but that, because she is herself a sinful creature, she can only bring forth another sinful creature like herself; and if a daughter, then a daughter inheriting all her own peculiar infirmities and disabilities." This quote is from *The Expositor's Bible, Volume 1*, page 316.

I discovered there were many other women I might have learned about, the ones who supported Jesus's ministry, his patrons who often traveled with him as recorded in the opening verses in Chapter 8 of Luke's gospel. "Now it happened that after this he made his way through towns and villages preaching and proclaiming the good news of the kingdom of God. With him went the twelve, as well as certain women who had been cured of evil spirits and ailments. Mary surnamed the Magdalene, from whom seven demons had gone out, Joanna the wife of Herod's steward Chuza, Susanna, and many others who provided for them out of their own resources." Wow, as a child I had only heard of the male followers.

At a time when a good Jew did not even acknowledge his sister if he saw her in the marketplace, Jesus not only spoke to but healed, taught women and welcomed them as part of his group.

What would I do with all this information? I kept going—that's what I did. I read what women theologians were writing and I continued individual therapy and joined one of Dr. Brown's therapy groups to vent my pain and anger. It would be many months before I reached what I believed to be the bottom line, namely fear and a deep sense of shame hidden beneath the anger. I had been struck on Chamblee Road by love and acceptance and it had led me through the wilderness only to find myself humbled by these two unwelcomed lodgers. Not feeling worthy as a wife and mother, not feeling good enough, smart enough, and not sure I could go on with what I felt God called me to do with the rest of my life. I was 42 years old. Faced now with the fear, and shame I had worked hard to deny for many years, the urge to quit school came to tempt me.

A poem written by an unknown woman touched me deeply as I read *Womanguides* by Rosemary Radford Ruether. It took me back to the experience on Chamblee Road in which the light of God broke through my depression and set me on the road to recovery.

You Are Enough!
A Woman Seminarian's Story

It is not enough
said her father
that you

>*get all A's each quarter*
>*play Mozart for your kinfolk*
>*win starred-firsts in contest*

you must
come home on your wedding night.

It is not enough
said her mother
that you

>*smile at Auntie Lockwood*
>*take cookies to the neighbors*
>*keep quiet while I'm napping*

you must
cure my asthma.

It is not enough
said her husband
that you

>*write letters to my parents*
>*fix pumpkin pie and pastry*
>*forget your name was Bauer*

you must
always
you must
never.

It is not enough
said her children
that you

> *make us female brownies*
> *tend our friends and puppies*
> *buy us Nike tennies*
> *you must*
> *let us kill you.*

It is not enough
said her pastor
that you

> *teach the second graders*
> *change the cloths and candles*
> *kneel prostrate at the altar*

as long as there are starving children in the world
you must
not eat
without guilt.

It is not enough
said her counselor
that you

> *struggle with the demons*
> *integrate your childhood*
> *leave when time is over*

you must
stop crying
clarify your poetic symbols
and
not feel
that you are not enough.

I give up
she said
I am not enough
and laid down
into the deep blue pocket
of night
to wait
for death

She waited . . .

and
finally
her heart exploded
her breathing stopped
They came with stretcher
took her clothes off
covered her with linen
then went away
and left her locked
in deep blue pocket tomb.
The voice said
   YOU ARE ENOUGH

       naked
       crying
       bleeding
       nameless
       starving
       sinful

YOU ARE ENOUGH

And on the third day
she sat up
  asked for milk and crackers
  took ritual bath with angels
  dressed herself with wings
and flew away.

Would she have to die to be free? It was clear some of her beliefs would need to die. At some point the anger subsided and what followed was a sense of sadness and loss that had been hidden beneath it. For me the answer was no, I would live. It was true the patriarchal system in the church had fostered and contributed to women's self-negation over the centuries. I had been taken in by a lie and yet I knew the Bible held truths that kept me coming back to its message of God's love for creation. I was little by little gaining what my heart longed for, a growing sense of self-acceptance of who I was at my deepest core along with freedom to live more fully.

After a total of eight years in school following the Chamblee Road experience, a Masters of Theology degree in hand and the completion of the ordination process, I was ordained a minister in the United Methodist Church and assigned to my first two churches, small ones in the Oak Cliff area of Dallas. At the service of ordination unexpected words came to thought, *I made it Momma.* The words surprised me. She had died years before. Even so I knew she had been a motivating factor in my accomplishment.

PART II

Emma

A reluctant grandmother.

CHAPTER 5

CARDAMOM MEMORIES

A decade had passed since the Chamblee Road experience, seminary and serving several churches, when Doug and I opened the door of a small coffee shop in Virrat, Finland, a village 60 miles north of Helsinki. Stepping inside, the scent of cardamom spice mingled with the strong aroma of brewed coffee swept over me. Accustomed to the robust smell of coffee, I hadn't encountered the intensely aromatic fragrance of the spice for decades. My reaction was immediate and visceral. My gut began churning as emotionally I was swept back in time as if caught up by the same tornado that carried Dorothy and Toto over the rainbow. This trip was not to the magical place of Oz, however, but to the land of contradiction, confusion and family secrets.

It was 1984 and I had come to Finland in search of my roots, hoping to find answers to long-standing questions about my maternal grandmother Lempi, Kylli my mother, and the man who might be my father. These questions had become a focus for me as I continued to work with Dr. Brown to unwind tangles of memories emerging in dreams and in experiences reminding me of my childhood. At the time I was an Associate Pastor at a church in Plano, Texas. Doug, who was an ardent devotee of his own family history, listened intently that day in the coffee shop as I put words on the memories that were leaping into consciousness. With the aroma of the crushed cardamom filling my nostrils, this vivid memory signaled the onset of discovery in the land of my ancestor's birth.

I was a young girl again, around the age of five or six, standing in Emma's pristine kitchen. Summer sunlight filtered through the white, starched curtains. I could almost hear the slapping *flop, flop* of her cooking slippers as she moved from pantry to Frigidaire to the red metal tabletop, laying out the needed ingredients for the metamorphosis about to take place.

Emma was married to my Grandpa but I was not to call her *grandma* because Momma said, "She's not your real grandmother."

I had some ideas about what *real* was. For instance, an old woman wearing a black, pointy hat and black cape didn't really fly around on her broom on Halloween. She wasn't real. Neither were talking animals or hairy monsters, droolers with red eyes and sharp claws that lived under my bed. Well, I wasn't absolutely sure about the things that might live under my bed. It did seem best, however, to follow the directions Momma gave me, so I just called this woman Emma. I wondered where my real grandmother might be.

Thursday was bread-baking day, and I always sat on a red padded kitchen chair that matched the tabletop. I knew to sit still even though I occasionally wiggled and kicked my feet under the table. My question to her was always the same, "Can I help?" It looked like such fun. Emma always said "no just be still and watch." Her long brown hair pinned behind her neck, her face devoid of make-up, she didn't talk as she moved through the ritual steps she knew so well. She seemed to be in a world uninhabited by me, perhaps back in the ancestral home of her youth.

Soon she was combining the silky, white flour with baking powder and soda, breaking the thin-shelled, brown eggs on the rim of the mixing bowl, adding milk, golden butter, the pungent cardamom, and the strange gray stuff that had begun to puff up as it waited its turn, the yeast. Emma created a large, round lump that landed with a *thud* when she threw it to the floured tabletop, then with resolute touch massaged and worked it until it was ready for its first rising. On some days she threw the dough down with such force I thought she must be mad at it. At those times I knew to be especially quiet and to keep my feet still. When the clump, soon braided into three well-formed loaves was placed in the oven, my taste buds kicked in, sending a rush of juices beneath my tongue. I could almost taste the luxuriant texture as it baked—the feel of the lightly browned crust in my mouth, the flavor of the cardamom, the sweetness of the crushed sugar cubes covering the top. The fragrance permeated the room, seeping into my clothes and hair.

Some things were a puzzle to me. How could Emma, who seemed so distant and cold, create something so grand? Maybe it had to do with her not being real. Maybe her *unrealness* was the reason I was never invited to snuggle in her lap while she read me a story or felt her hand stroking my blond hair or saw a smile that said unmistakably, *I love you, Katie.* Even so, I loved Emma and I wanted her to love me, too.

Tears surfaced along with the memories that surfaced that day at the coffee shop in the small village of Virrat, Finland. Both became an open door for much more to come.

CHAPTER 6

HOPED FOR BUT
UNEXPECTED MEETINGS

We had few expectations of finding relatives or information about my family of origin as we drove the short distance to the only hotel in Virrat. Sue, our travel agent, hoped the call she had made some weeks before would mean a room was waiting for us in the Tarjani Hotel, even though she had found no one there who spoke English. Neither had there been a response to the letter she had written telling of my desire to find family connections.

"It doesn't look promising," Sue told me. "Even though English is taught in Finnish schools, Virrat is a small place, you know. Good luck."

Not knowing we were in for a big surprise, Doug and I climbed the short flight of stairs to the hotel lobby and walked toward a mustached man who looked up and smiled warmly. He stood behind a wooden counter, a portion of which could be raised to serve as a pass-through, and greeted us.

"Good afternoon," he said, extending his hand as he spoke. "I am Johan Erkilla, the proprietor. You must be the DeGrows."

He not only spoke English, but, we learned, taught it at Helsinki University. He had not been in the hotel the day the travel agent called and expressed regret for not responding to Sue's letter introducing us. As Doug signed the register, our host left me speechless with a litany of steps he had taken on our behalf.

"I have contacted some of your relatives. One is coming in by bus from Tampere this evening. Tomorrow, cousins will be at the summer cottage that was once your grandfather's bakery. I have arranged for someone to meet you and take you there at nine tomorrow. A genealogist, Mr. Jarvi, will be here at four this afternoon to give you some initial information and, if you desire, be available to do further research."

By now, totally surprised and a bit overwhelmed, tears welled up as I thanked Johan with words inadequate to express what I felt.

As it turned out, tears would be my companion during the next week as I met cousins and second cousins, some of whom resembled my mother and me. Together we walked a short distance from the former bakery to the abandoned farmhouse that was long ago the home of my ancestors. Through the help of our interpreter I dared make a request for the old key still in the front door. The owner, to my regret, vigorously shook her head as she responded. "If I give her the key, how will I lock the door?"

I didn't laugh, but could have. The window panes were broken out and a back entry was without a door. Even though it seemed so right for me to have the key, I came to terms with the denial quickly and commented to Doug, "I will just have to conclude that a woman in Finland has a key that belongs to me."

Several hours later, while we continued our visit with relatives at the cottage, a man drove up in an aging pick-up truck, walked briskly to where we were sitting in lawn chairs and spoke to my cousin. He then stood and waited for our host to interpret his message to me, "The owner of the farm has changed her mind and would like you to have the key. Would you please go with him to receive it?"

Doug, the interpreter, and I left immediately to claim my prize. I later learned how the villagers had intervened on my behalf. Word had quickly circulated of the owner's refusal to give me the key, which resulted in a scolding for *her ungracious response to the woman who came all the way from America to see her ancestors' farm.* Feeling the cool metal in my hand, I pictured my mother as a little girl, turning it in the lock. I thought she would like my having it.

Beautifully crafted letters stored in the attic of the former bakery were now in my possession as well.

Grandpa had written them to his love, Lempi Elizabeth, my grandmother, and the sweet words and tender poetry must have stirred a response in her as they now did in me. I had never before seen this side of my grandfather. Puzzled as to how the letters came to be in Finland when the street address on the envelopes was Lenox Avenue with the postmark, "New York City," my cousin Maire explained, "After Lempi's death, her younger sister Emma went to America to marry your grandfather and raise your mother. They came back to Finland in the 1920s, bringing your mother, who was then about 11. They stayed for a few years before returning to the United States."

I had not heard this part of Momma's history before.

"This cottage was originally your grandfather's bakery," my cousin reiterated. This explained the huge stone oven that dominated one corner of the cottage where we were enjoying yet another cup of coffee. "Your grandfather likely brought the letters back with him," my cousin continued. "They have been waiting for you all this time."

She then handed me a photograph she had retrieved from the same trunk, a picture taken in 1910. I finally saw Lempi gazing back at me in all her simple elegance— her high-necked, white dress with sleeves pushed up above the elbows, revealing strong arms and hands, her light brown hair parted in the middle, full around her face. There she was, standing next to my handsome, seated grandfather, one hand on his shoulder. And there was Momma, too, a precious, healthy-looking baby girl. I wept. Several cousins who said they remembered stories about Lempi also wiped away tears. I wondered if they were moved by my feelings or sad because of their own memories. I was left to wonder.

I was left to wonder about something else as well. When I was young and had asked Momma about my real grandmother Lempi, she told me she died on the very day she was born, in childbirth. If this was a picture of Lempi along with Grandpa and Momma, that could not be true. I chose not to ask about this with my new-found relatives but would be sure to explore it further when working with Mr. Jarvi, the genealogist.

My thoughts returned to the memories that had surfaced earlier in the day in the small coffee shop, recalling my time on the red padded kitchen chair, watching Emma bake the cardamom bread. Secrets hovered like stale air in summer back then, secrets I was now beginning to uncover. It would be many years before learning the full extent of them. For now it was enough to delight in my newly-discovered family and enjoy my coffee along with a thick, buttery slice of Finnish bread. This time together was not the last kindness shown me that day.

As Doug and I began our good-byes, my cousin Maire added, "Oh, by the way, your mother had a cousin living in the Detroit area who could tell you about Lempi. She is quite elderly, but you might want to contact her." Her name is Lily.

Grandmother Lempi, Grandpa, and Momma
A beautiful family.

CHAPTER 7

THE GRANDMOTHER I NEVER KNEW

Four o'clock rolled around, time to return to the hotel for the meeting with the genealogist that had been arranged by the proprietor. Mr. Jarvi was a pleasant man with white hair, bright blue eyes, like those of so many Finns, and a pleasant smile. He provided enough information on my grandmother Lempi to increase my interest in her story. One discrepancy between his research and what I had been told by Momma was obvious, the date of Lempi's death was listed as 1913 when Momma was 3 years old. Momma had indeed adjusted her story to meet her needs, whatever they were. Lily Salo, the cousin Maire had mentioned earlier in the day was also included. I would definitely make an effort to reach her when I returned home but not before I began my own search for information at the library and on the internet.

One definition of the term "fact" found in Webster's Dictionary is *something that has actual existence*. Lempi Elizabeth Korvela began taking on reality to me as more facts came to light. Born August 8, 1888 on a farm in northern Finland, she was only 18 when she left her homeland. What stories had she heard about the promised land of America? Had she seen pictures of the Statue of Liberty with her torch held high? Miss Liberty had settled in her place on Ellis Island only 20 short years before Lempi would see her. What would the immigration process be like? These questions would not be answered with certainty though I could surmise the answers from many other immigrants who wrote of their experiences. To this day, when I see the old photographs of the *huddled masses yearning to breathe free*, I look for her youthful face.

On the one hand, Lempi's life appeared to be like millions of others who have come to these shores. Its uniqueness lies in the fact that she was an individual with a narrative never to be repeated in exactly the same way, as is the case with all of us.

Some might consider it luck that led me to her story. I call it Grace. While growing up, her name was seldom heard but as my research continued I found we were alike in many ways. She was impelled to leave the familiar for tangible reasons: ongoing conflict and war with a powerful neighbor, Russia. She also knew what hunger meant, even to the point of seeing people starve during periods of famine. My own research turned up the fact that she was one of over a quarter-million Finns arriving on American soil between 1900 and 1920, looking not for streets of gold but freedom and food to sustain them. As a child keenly aware of World War II, I struggled to find order and nurture in a family unable or motivated to provide much of either. Lempi made a physical journey across a vast and, at times, turbulent ocean. I made an internal one in an attempt to create order out of chaos and make sense of my perceptions. As with her, the *waters* were rough at times.

The church had a major impact on Lempi, as it did on all Finns in her day. In fact, it dominated every aspect of life. Membership was not optional in Finland's National Lutheran Church, and no one could marry without permission from the clergy or apply for a job without a confirmation certificate. She had to obtain a document attesting to her good character before receiving the government passport to immigrate to America. The required 10-percent tithe to the church was a hardship for her parents, who had nine children to feed and clothe. Her first contact with a church organization in the United States would result in another life-changing event. Weekly get-togethers for immigrants were held on Friday evenings at the Salvation Army on Lenox Avenue in New York City. Lempi decided to go. So did another young Finn, her future husband, Mauri Johannes Mettenan. I wonder how many unions resulted from those *angels of mercy* who were doing their part in welcoming newcomers and helping them transition into

American citizens. And how ironic that when growing up I had attended events for needy children at the Salvation Army in my hometown of Kalamazoo, Michigan, and on occasion received food and clothing as well.

Was Lempi surprised by the compassion shown her and the many immigrants who passed through their doors?

CHAPTER 8

LILY SALO

Having returned home the time seemed right to begin my search for Lily Salo, Momma's cousin whom I had learned of while in Finland. My search for her address was successful, I wrote her and she in turn, had promptly answered the letter I sent and invited me to her home in suburban Detroit. I had mentioned my desire to talk about my Grandmother Lempi and my mother. Lily made no reference to such a conversation in her return letter, but I remained hopeful. Doug and I made plans to visit Michigan and flew into the Detroit Metro Airport a few months later.

The houses on the tree-lined streets in Lily's neighborhood were small and well cared for. They resembled ones found in many parts of the country built right after World War II: small, with two bedrooms and a separate one-car garage at the end of a dirt driveway. I felt excitement as we parked and started up the short walkway from the curb. She must have been watching for us as she was at the door before we stepped onto the porch. Greeting us warmly, she unlocked the screen door and invited us in. She was short, maybe five foot two, with gentle features and a ready smile. I felt an immediate liking for her. Soon we were seated in her snug living room and being served coffee and a plate of home-baked cookies.

Lily showed great interest in our trip to Finland and asked about specific people with whom she had had some contact over the years. "My father and your grandfather were very close, you know," she said. I hadn't heard this before and enjoyed her recollections of the two brothers. She clearly liked reminiscing and added stories of her early days in this country. One of her biggest surprises had been the abundance of food in America. "When I arrived in America in 1908, I did not find streets lined with gold but rather with food. Food seemed to be everywhere in New York City. There were so many street vendors. And I'll bet you can't guess what I came to like, oysters and clams. Those were big sellers then. Another thing I remember, 'penny licks.' For a penny you could get a lick of ice cream from a glass cup. I always tried to get the first lick before others had a turn," Lily laughed, and Doug and I enjoyed her stories.

When the time seemed right to ask about my grandmother, I began, carefully picking my words.

"Lily, our relatives in Finland gave me a picture of

Lempi, my grandfather and my mother," I began tentatively as I took the picture from my bag and carefully removed the covering I had used to protect it. "I wasn't able to get much information from the relatives about her, as mentioned in my letter. I'm in hopes you can tell me about her."

Taking the picture in her hands, she sighed. "It's a sad story about Lempi," she began. "Are you sure you want to hear it?" I looked across at Doug who gave me a reassuring look as he put his coffee cup down on an end table.

I held my breath. "I am sure, Lily. Would you tell me about her?" After a pause, she began.

"Your grandfather came to America first. He got a job in New York City working on the docks as a stevedore. When Lempi came she found work as a maid in some rich people's house. Finnish maids were in high demand then you know. She and your grandpa met at an immigrant party at the Salvation Army Church.

I nodded without mentioning I already knew about their meeting.

"The center was on Lenox Avenue, close to where Lempi worked. I went to some of those parties myself when I came to America. They were a nice way to meet people from the old country.

"What I was told is that Lempi and your Grandfather Mauri courted for quite a while, then got married and moved to Michigan. The Model T Ford was just coming out, and your grandpa got a job in one of their first factories here in Detroit. Your mother was born, and then another little girl, Tuovi, came soon after. It wasn't long before I heard that Lempi was pregnant again. I don't know, maybe another baby was more than she could...," Lily's words trailed off and we sat in silence, the only sound the ticking of a clock. "She had an abortion and died within a few days," Lily said. "That was back in 1913."

Silence once again.

My mind scurried over the recollection I had had while in Finland of Momma telling me her mother died when she was born. I knew Momma was born in 1910, making her three years old when her mother died. Wouldn't she have been old enough to remember her? Lily went on to say that Momma's little sister Tuovi died a few months later.

"Your mother was left with your grandfather. He was like a crazy man, depressed and drinking heavily. His grief nearly destroyed him."

Lily had said it was a very sad story. She was right. My eyes brimmed with tears, tears I hoped Lily would not notice. Seeing them she might decide not to continue. Ironically, I wondered if what she had shared was too much for her. Nonetheless, she continued.

"After Lempi died, Emma, her younger sister, was sent here from Finland. She was just 15 years old and didn't want to come to the States. But that was the tradition in those days. She had to come because of your mother. If Lempi hadn't left a child, Emma would not have been sent here. "Emma resented it. I always heard that she took it out on your mother, treating her badly."

My early perception of Emma's feelings about Momma, Grandpa and me were probably on target. She didn't seem to like us much. Now I wondered if she simply hadn't been able to overcome her anger or sadness at being sent from Finland to this country. Fifteen, after all, is a pretty tender age to make such a voyage against her wishes.

Lily continued, "Your mother had trouble in school, and they thought she wasn't smart enough to learn. I don't know. When I was around her, she just seemed unhappy."

I knew Momma had only finished third grade and couldn't read or write very well. Did she have a learning disability? Was she depressed? These questions were not asked in our culture at that time in history. People with such problems might be tagged as feeble-minded or defective, but depressed or suffering from learning disabilities? No.

The three of us sat quietly for a time, each processing the words that had been spoken. I had wanted to know my history and, as I might have expected, discovered family secrets in the process. What would I learn next? I would be led to my own memories of growing up to find answers.

Lily and I corresponded for a time until she sold her home and moved into a nursing facility. She died at the ripe old age of 92. I continue to be thankful for her.

Momma

Momma in 1942.

CHAPTER 9

WHAT'S WRONG WITH MOMMA?

She's mentally challenged, I thought, as I introduced myself to the woman who took the only empty chair at the table next to me. She had come with her father to the coffee shop for a monthly book discussion. It was the first time for both of us. Something about her reminded me of my mother. My emotional reaction to her made it difficult for me to keep my thoughts focused on the book the group had all read and were there to discuss.

It had been decades since being with Momma but here I was like a child again, uneasy, even tense, with protective feelings welling up in me. It was as if Momma, not a fellow book club visitor, was sitting there with me sipping coffee. After an hour and a half I was happy to be on the road again heading for the comforts of home.

Being in my safe place did not stop the floodgate that seemed to have opened, memories and feelings rising from my shadowy unconscious into consciousness. Taking out a collage of photographs, pictures of Momma and me, I settled in to inspect the small black and white snap shots sent to me by my aunt. Prior to her thoughtful gift I had not any visual reminders of childhood. Small cracks had covered the surface of a few pictures and others, dim from age, did not deter me in my search for clues as to how I thought and felt back then.

Carefully examining the first image at about six months, bundled up in a snow suit, looking away from the camera with bottom lip pushed out as if ready to cry, *restricted* was the word that came to mind. It would have been hard for me to move with so much clothing. Then more pictures, the language of the body speaking from across the decades. Several taken when I was four or five, appearing anxious, with fingers at my mouth or clutched in front of me in small, balled up fists with Momma hovering over me. I stood in her shadow. Another one I have named, *my happy child,* taken in my kindergarten class at Harding Elementary School.

Momma had been an attractive woman in her early years, with blond hair and pretty blue-green eyes. No smiles were present in her pictures, nothing to suggest she was enjoying herself. A more concrete reason may have been the cause for her solemnity. As far back as I can remember she had no front teeth. She wore a strange sort of partial to hide her loss, a kind I have not seen since. It was made of thin wire with little spaces where cotton could be inserted creating "cotton teeth." Each day I would watch her pull off small tufts from a fat cotton ball, carefully shape each piece and then press them one by one into the spaces of the wire fixture. The partial and a warm evening in the summer at Gourdneck Lake are forever linked in memory to an early attempt to help Momma, the first of many failures.

Our swim, actually more of a 'splashing around in shallow water,' started out just fine. Kingfisher birds skimmed the water retrieving small minnows, Purple Martins, nesting in bird boxes that Grandpa had constructed and set on high poles, began their nightly ritual, swooping and diving for the goodly supply of insects. The water, in contrast to the air, had felt cool on my feet and when I stepped in next to the pier. Then it happened. Momma's reaction to the difference in temperature was to sneeze causing the partial to fly out of her mouth into the water. She looked stricken and began searching the area in which it fell. "I'll help, Momma," I said as I reached my small arm into the dreaded sea weed I was sure held all manner of scary things. "Don't worry, I'll find it." She gave me no response but moaned and was in obvious distress. We continued searching for some time without success, my words of assurance soon becoming an annoyance to her. She became angry at my little girl attempts. Then I cried. I had not been able to help.

The tale of the lost partial became a family story that evoked laughter in listeners, with the exception of Momma and me. It was a big loss for her and, while I did not have words for my feelings, I knew I didn't like Tony Momma's husband, Emma, Grandpa, my aunt and uncle talking and laughing at the story. I scowled, yelled for them to stop or covered my ears. I believed they were teasing Momma. There was an additional reason. I had already figured out when Momma was upset I might be the recipient of her harsh treatment. There could be a scolding, or worse yet, a spanking in store for me.

The jumble of feelings that grabbed me by surprise at the coffee shop earlier in the evening could now be identified. Anger, fear and a sense of helplessness rose up in my throat until I felt like a container too full for its contents. *Later*, I thought, *I will deal with this another time*. It wasn't to be. Much of the night was spent wrestling with the long-buried feelings and disjointed memories. The last hour before daybreak the thought came to take the photographs to show Dr. Brown. I was still seeing her occasionally and would make an appointment to do just that. I wanted to share them with someone I trusted when I talked about Momma's problems, one of whom was the man she married.

Momma and Me
Standing in her shadow.

Tony

The non-conformist.

CHAPTER 10

TONY

Tony's image was clear in the photograph I handed to Dr. Brown. He stood with his arms crossed in front of him, wearing a white shirt with the rolled up sleeves, smiling with his mouth closed. He likely smiled this way to hide a mouth minus teeth just as Momma usually did.

"Tell me about him," Dr. Brown said.

My thoughts were clear since I had written about him in my journal after receiving the photos.

"I was not to call him Daddy. *He is not your daddy.* Momma's voice would ring out with parental authority if I ever forgot to call her husband, 'Tony'. Nothing was new about this since I had also learned to call Emma by her first name rather than 'Grandma'. She was not my real grandmother and Tony was not my real father. Hmm. I had yet to grasp the meaning of all this.

Tony had come to America from the Netherlands

when he was nine years old. As the baby of the large family and his father's favorite, he'd held a place of honor. According to stories told to me by several of his cousins I tracked down after returning from Finland, unless Tony wanted to do something, he was not required to do it. Since he didn't like school, his frequent absences meant he had little formal education to provide him with opportunities as an adult.

My imaginings about him included the belief that he grew up poor. We seemed to be, so as a child I naturally drew that conclusion. Nothing could have been farther from the truth. His father, Anthony, for whom he was named, had been a diamond merchant in Belgium and the Netherlands, buying and selling the precious stones and becoming rich in the process.

Arriving with his family in Kalamazoo, where fellow Dutchmen had come before him, the senior Anthony settled on the west side of the city and built a fine two-story house with a wide porch across the front and along one side. The house had been pointed out to me several times but I never entered it or sat in one of the chairs on the porch. Momma said Tony's parents disowned him because he was a "bum." Bum was a new and funny word to me. I liked it and said it a lot until Momma told me to stop. I didn't know what "disowned" meant either but supposed it had something to do with not liking Tony.

Once, Momma, Tony and I went to the house because we needed money and Tony was going to make an appeal to his father for help. Momma and I were to stay in a big yard in back of the house while Tony talked to his father. If things went well, he would call us and we could come in to meet his parents. I played in the grass while we waited then suddenly felt a sharp pain in the palm of my right hand. I yelped and jumped around before seeing the big bee that had stung me. I knew Momma felt sorry for me and tried to help by tying her hanky around my hand, which was growing bigger and redder by the minute. The first aid didn't seem to help and my tears continued.

Tony looked mad when he came to get us and I stopped crying. His father would not give him any money and so we left. I didn't get to meet his mother and father but Momma told me they weren't my real grandparents anyway so it didn't matter.

Tony was different from anyone else I knew. He didn't go to work every day and didn't stay on one job very long. Instead he had lots of different ones. Momma called him a "shyster." I didn't know what that word meant either, but I learned it had to do with tricking people. He also asked people he didn't even know to give him money. Lots of times they did.

Once, Momma and I went with him to a car dealership on South Westnedge Avenue. Lots of new cars filled a parking lot, and one even sat inside a big room with glass windows all around it. Tony told the man who worked there he was interested in buying a new car. Could he take one for a trial run before he decided? We took one from the parking lot for a road test, but he didn't take it back. This meant we had a new car for a few days until the dealership man tracked him down. He had given a last name like "Smith" or "Jones" and a non-existent address. I still remember one pretty light blue and green Kaiser Frazer parked in the driveway of our apartment house for over a week with neighbors coming by to admire it.

Then another time we might have had a new couch if I hadn't been so smart. Momma, Tony and I went to Vermuellen's Furniture store on the corner of Rose Street one Saturday morning to look at their furniture. I was delighted with my first visit to such a huge room full of couches, overstuffed chairs and others items for the home. I bounced about from couch to couch while Tony talked with a salesman. Momma kept her eye on me but didn't tell me to stop what I was doing so I continued enjoying myself. After a time I hopped my way to a desk near the back of the store to hear what Tony and the man were talking about. Getting there just as the man sat down and began to write on a long sheet of paper I heard him ask, "What is your name and address?" I didn't know the address but I knew our name and could even spell it. "VanDeWouwer," I declared. "Capital V a-n, Capital D e, Capital W o-u-w-e-r, VanDeWouwer." Whoops. A bad look came over Tony's face and the man at the desk just put his pen down and shook his head. Momma took my hand and hurried me out of the store while Tony followed close behind.

He spanked me when we were outside. I didn't like it

one bit and let him know with my screams over the injustice of the matter. Having no idea what I had done wrong, I decided to never spell a word for him again.

Other people seemed to like Tony. He had an easy way about him, liked to tell jokes and laugh, and made friends wherever he went. People gave him nick names like *Pasquale* and *Luigi*. I don't know why. Maybe it was because they were popular Italian names, and he had some Italian friends. He had a nick name for me too. It was *kid*. I didn't like him calling me that. I had a name. Other people called me Katie or Katherine.

Tony said words that I learned were not good for me to say, ones that would get me in trouble. I wondered about the way he was and thought for a while he would just rather have a good time than work. Then I concluded he was not very smart. I never saw him read a book or write anything. He really was different from any other person I have known.

Tony stories took up most of the time with Dr. Brown that day. Before I left her office she suggested I think about his influence on me before we met again. I had given this subject a good bit of thought and would have some answers for her.

Even though we weren't close I believed he had a big impact on me. Since he seemed to get in trouble a lot I decided at a young age to be different from him. I would not ask people for money. I would get a job and work hard. I would tell the truth as I had been taught to do in school, and I would call people by their real names.

CHAPTER 11

A POLKA DOT DRESS

Momma was wearing a navy blue dress with white polka dots and buttons down the front, along with two small ribbons just beneath the collar. She often wore a small artificial rose near the top button. I had forgotten how much Momma liked wearing flowers. Her life was sad in many ways, and yet she often added this small touch of beauty to an otherwise plain outfit. *Good for her*, I thought. Looking at the picture immediately reminded me of a time long ago when she also wore the polka dot dress along with a pink rose.

Momma's formal education was said to have ended in the third grade. "They said I couldn't learn," she had told me. I believed her but wondered why. What was wrong with her? Clearly ill at ease in social settings, not making eye contact with others but rather looking at the person's shoulder or beyond them into space, I recalled a time when she and I both were uncomfortable in a group setting.

The girls in my second grade class were to join their mothers for a coffee at my classmate Virginia Clark's house. Each of us made an invitation to take home with the necessary information along with the initials R.S.V.P., which, we were told, meant our mothers should let Virginia's mother know if we were coming. We were to arrive at 3:30 p.m. right after school. The purpose of the event was for mothers to get acquainted and discuss ways to support our education. Momma said she would come.

On the day of the party my stomach felt growly and upset whenever I thought about being there. Momma was unpredictable when she became troubled or nervous. I feared she might be too loud or get mad about something. Then I wondered if the other mothers would be nice to her. What if she said something they didn't like? At such times I could be overwhelmed with a feeling not yet given a name, embarrassment. Would I feel it today and would Momma get upset at the party?

It was a beautiful spring day with tulips peeking out of the moist Michigan dirt and white puffy clouds skittering overhead. Leaving through the side door of school I could see Momma waiting as she said she would be. She looked nice in her polka dot dress, her red platform shoes and a small hat with prongs on either side to hold it in place. Her blond hair peeked from beneath it as if too shy to show itself. She was nervous, I could tell, and I felt nervous too.

In less than 10 minutes we entered the Clark's neat living room. We girls were directed to sit on the floor in front of where our mothers were seated. After introductions cups of coffee or glasses of milk were handed to each of us and then a full plate of oatmeal cookies was passed around. Soon our progress in school became the subject of discussion. Ethel's mom commented on the books being used for teaching arithmetic. She said they were exceptionally good. Margaret's mother said she encouraged her daughter to get her homework done soon after she got home in the afternoon. Her chores came afterward. Things were going well when Momma made an effort to join in the conversation. Her words, as usual, seemed to be directed toward someone out in space.

"I don't ask my girl to help me do housework. I want her to do her school work and get good report cards." I held my breath. *Oh, please don't say any more, Momma,* hoping she would somehow get my silent message. My stomach started doing flip flops. It turned out to be the only thing she contributed to the conversation because several mothers responded without hesitation.

"But you know she needs to learn how to take care of a house, to clean and cook, not just do schoolwork."

Heads nodded in agreement. "After all she will get married one day and will need to know how to cook and clean."

Momma looked down at her feet while her face turned a shade of red. I felt angry, wanting to tell the other mothers to leave her alone. *She's trying hard to be nice and talk like the rest of you,* I thought to myself. I wanted the party to end even though I dreaded what might come afterward. When she was upset and unwilling to be comforted by my feeble efforts, Momma could spew out her pain in words that left me bereft. Always the same ones, words I understood to mean she didn't want me when I was a baby. *I wanted to get rid of you, but they wouldn't let me. I wanted to leave you at the hospital, but my dad wouldn't let me.* Would this be one of those days? I readied myself for the possibility by telling myself Momma didn't mean it. She really didn't mean it. She would just get mad. Despite this I always tried to fight back tears when hearing the dreaded words, usually without success. On more than one occasion I would mull over Momma's words about wanting to leave me at the hospital. Were there people who took care of babies who are left? I had never heard of children who grew up in a hospital. Later I learned about orphanages.

The party finally ended with polite expressions of thanks and a mention of doing this again in the fall. Then the girls led the way out to the front porch jostling a bit for a turn on the swing at one end. I waited to hold Momma's hand until we reached the corner and crossed the road on the way to our apartment on Walnut Street. That day her anger was directed more at the mothers than at me.

"Don't ever ask me to come to another one of those stupid coffees. Those women think they are so smart and know everything. What do they know?" I nodded and said I didn't like them either, feeling relieved that this time her anger was not directed at me.

My Grandfather, Maurice Metsa
and Momma, Kylli

CHAPTER 12

GRANDPA METSA

Grandpa stood over six feet tall, and his gruff voice matched his heavy-set build. His hands fascinated me as a young girl. Two fingers were missing from his right hand and one from his left. He'd lost them in farming accidents back in Finland. I never had the courage to ask him what my little girl mind wanted to know about these accidents—like what happened, what did you do with the fingers, do you miss them? His hair was the same color as Momma's and mine, "dishwater blond," as it was called then, and he had a matching mustache. He smoked Lucky Strike cigarettes, and when he cleared his throat every morning, all within hearing distance shuddered. I loved Grandpa—and I also feared him.

A complex man, he could shed tears when hearing a sad story but would easily ignore the pain of those around him. He was a gentle soul when it came to caring for wild birds and flowers, and yet, despite my shrieks of protest, he once put a litter of unwanted kittens in a gunnysack and dropped them in Gourdneck Lake.

Unlike Emma, Grandpa told stories of the old days, usually after consuming sizable amounts of alcohol. A twice-yearly visit from his brother, Charlie, became predictable. They drank, told stories and sang songs from their youth. Emma was agitated days before Charlie's arrival but, nevertheless, took the necessary steps in preparation for the visit, including stocking the Frigidaire with plenty of beer, filling the pantry with food and firing up the sauna. I felt excited about the stories I would hear.

Grandpa usually started first on the litany of tales, including the pledges he had made before boarding the ship for the United States in 1906. He vowed to find work other than farming, to avoid contact with "Ruskies," and to stay out of churches. It didn't matter that I had heard the stories before and knew what would come next. It was like reading a favorite book until I knew it by heart and still found it magical.

"Before I came to this country I decided I wouldn't plant anything but flowers in my garden," Grandpa reminisced. "Farming was too much work with too many failures."

Poor soil, the weather that ruined crops, insects that ate the work of his hands before it could be harvested; no, he was through tilling the soil. It had failed to support his family on more than a few occasions. He was tired of being hungry and seeing the weakest among his countrymen die during periods of famine. Then, too, farms were passed down to the oldest son and that wasn't Grandpa. He heard that jobs were plentiful in America, and he promised himself he would find good-paying work but not as a farmer.

"This family has never gone hungry and it never will while I am alive," he would remind us at the end of this particular recitation. By this time he had risen from his chair beside Charlie and gone to the metal wash tub filled with beer bottles. Opening one with the bottle opener hooked on to a long piece of twine, he continued with his story.

"I went right to work in this country unloading cargo on the docks of New York City. "Then I heard about some of the men moving out here to Michigan because the Model T car was the big thing. Later I got a job as a sheet metal worker with Fischer Body and, by God, I made a good living."

Brother Charlie nodded vigorously at this point in the story. He, too, had found a job in the auto industry in Detroit. They were both doing well.

When I again heard the term "Ruskies," I knew Grandpa was moving to the second part of story time. Russian people were among his shipmates on the voyage to America. They were in the long lines at the arrival centers and at the Salvation Army, where the immigrants were sent for social services. Despite these contacts, he held on to his loathing of them with a tight grasp. I had never seen a Ruskie and fantasized a rough-looking character that would likely scare me. What was Grandpa's prejudice about? It stemmed from the repeated conflicts between Finns and Russians over the years.

"Their armies wouldn't leave us alone. They wanted our land. Once they had it, they drafted our boys and young men. They had no right."

His voice cracked when he told of his older brother and father dying of starvation in a Russian detention camp. The men had been part of a Finnish fighting group called the White Forces and were captured after one of the Russian invasions. By this time Charlie was usually crying while Grandpa continued his tirade, clenching his fists and bellowing out his damnation of their eastern neighbor. His actions were almost as frightening to me as the imagined Ruskies but, despite this, his stories fascinated me.

Why did Grandpa loathe church? I knew the story nearly by heart. Finland had a state church, the National Lutheran Church. Grandpa said that meant it was allowed a tax from the Finnish people, 10 percent of their income. As was true for other poor farmers, this was a hardship for Grandpa's family. In the spring of his last year in his homeland an official from the church came for his family's much-valued cow because his family could not pay the church tax.

"No church for me. I've never put my foot in one and I never will."

By this time in the storytelling, his anger had subsided and there was sadness in his eyes. Time for a decision on my part: if I ever went to church it would probably be best not to tell him. I did wonder what the Lutheran Church in Finland did with the cow.

As the evening went on, there would be more storytelling with eating and talking until the singing began. We had moved from the kitchen to the living room, which was located in the upper level of the house. Several neighbors arrived with accordions. I didn't understand all the Finnish words but could tell whether they were happy or sad songs. Both Grandpa and Charlie cried some more, even during the happy songs. As for me, the music took me to a soft place inside where I felt happy and contented.

Emma always left the room several times during storytelling to check the sauna. It was being readied for the traditional Finnish bath near the end of the evening. The sauna was connected to the kitchen by a small hallway. This was quite an innovation since the ones in Finland were not in the houses themselves, but close to them, outside. The walls were made of gray stone and the wooden slats in the floor and benches on one side made it a room like none other I had seen. It was a fascinating place for me.

To ready the sauna the small stove in the middle was fired up, sending out intense heat when its heavy door was opened. Two gray metal dippers with long handles lay on a bench next to a pail of water. These would be used to throw water on the rock walls which in turn created great clouds of steam. Willow branches from trees near the lake were used as switches to beat our skin. I wasn't sure why we did that, but it was supposed to be good for us, something about circulation. Women and children went first before the room had grown too hot. The men were last. I wondered how Grandpa and Charlie could keep singing while taking a sauna when I could barely breathe.

I liked all the stories I heard on those party nights except for one Momma told me about things that happened before I was born. She said when Grandpa drank too much and people had gone home she and Emma would sometimes hide from him. "He would get mean and hit us if he found us. He would go out the front door, go around the house and back in the kitchen door, then do it all over again until he got so tired he would go to his bed and sleep." I asked Momma where she and Emma hid but she wouldn't tell me. Guess she wanted to keep her secret in case she ever needed to hide again. Hearing this story was the only part of the evening I didn't like.

Thinking back I realized no mention of my Grandmother Lempi was made on those party nights or at any other time for that matter. Grandpa never so much as spoke her name, but she was his wife and I think he must have loved her. I thought little of it at the time. Lempi didn't seem to exist as far as the stories went.

CHAPTER 13

THE BIBLE 101

Grandpa's anger at the church led to expected results: no one in my family went to church nor owned a Bible. No access to either often led to a misunderstanding of the few Bible stories I'd heard, like the one about Jesus's birth and the Santa Claus tale. I thought Bethlehem was located at the North Pole. My love affair with the Bible would officially begin in 3rd grade.

Each morning, after pledging our allegiance to the flag, we heard verses from the Psalms, followed by a story. (A brief aside to the reader: I in no way am suggesting we go back to reading the Bible in school. It was just the way it was then). I loved the idea of God as a kind shepherd in Psalm 23 but it was the stories that captured my imagination most, especially the ones about Moses. Imagine hearing an angel that spoke to him from inside a burning bush. When Moses saw the bush he said, "I think I'll stop and look at this." It was a good thing he did because it was God talking to him and He wanted Moses to lead the Hebrew people out of slavery. Moses didn't think he could do it but God said He would be with him to help. So the Hebrews left Egypt for the Promised Land. They moved—I could imagine that because Momma, Tony and I moved a lot but never to a promised land, at least not that I knew of. We usually moved when the rent was due and home was always another sparsely furnished apartment or cheap hotel room. I was happy enough if the new place had a radio so I could listen to *Arthur Godfrey Time, Let's Pretend* and The *Lone Ranger.* I loved listening to the radio almost as much as going to the Saturday movies. Stories, in any form, fascinated me and I was learning that the Bible was full of them.

One day I asked my friend Ethel about Moses. Wanting to learn more and knowing she could tell me because she went to the Greek Orthodox Church every Sunday morning, she said her parents were born in Greece, which was near Jesus's birthplace. There went my theory of the North Pole. *Was Greek the same as Hebrew?* Ethel didn't know but said she'd ask her mother. She did and they weren't. So between the readings in school and Ethel I received my basic information about the Bible. It still wasn't enough. What better place to hear the stories than in church? I decided to go the very next Sunday even though Grandpa didn't like churches.

At that time we were living on Walnut Street near a church with colored glass windows. Sometimes I stopped to look at them on my way home from school and one afternoon I walked up the concrete steps and pulled the handle on one of the big front doors. To my surprise, it opened. Cautiously stepping inside, I looked around the long hall that ran across the back and saw a carved wooden table. On it were two white candles in tall, shiny holders, and golden plates stacked one on another. A coat rack on the opposite wall included a space for umbrellas. Two black ones rested in the openings. Swinging doors were on either side of the table, one of which I slowly pushed opened to look inside. "Wow." The light coming through the glass windows made them sparkle with colors—red, purple, gold and green. They were the most beautiful windows I had ever seen.

The most amazing sight was a window at the front showing a man in a ship. The waves were hitting the boat like they did sometimes on Gourdneck Lake when there was a storm. The man was holding the ship's wheel with both hands but he didn't look scared. He looked wonderful to me. I was pretty sure it was Jesus and I was right. At the bottom of the heavy, brown frame were the words, *Jesus, Savior, Pilot Me.* This was where I would come to church on Sunday.

I quietly left the building, taking with me the memory of the beautiful glass, pausing just long enough to read the sign in front. It said the service on Sunday was at 10:00 a.m. and the title of the sermon was, *Where Are*

You Going? Momma didn't mind when I told her about wanting to go to church. She didn't offer to take me either and that was fine. Our apartment was close by so the next Sunday morning she just said to come home right afterward.

Sunday came, and I was excited to hear a story. After arriving in plenty of time, I found a good seat in the third row in front of the place where the preacher was sitting, spread my skirt neatly on my knees and looked around. The song books were in small, wooden boxes hooked on the backs of the seats and page numbers were listed on a board behind the organ. Finding them right away, but disappointed at not knowing the songs, when the time came to sing I did the best I could. In a while a woman in a long black dress stood next to the organ to sing alone. It was called a solo. I didn't like it much. She sounded screechy and her voice made me shiver. Then the preacher got in his high up place to talk. I didn't like him either.

The story he told scared me. It was about a time when stars would fall from the sky and people would be fighting with each other, and the city would be burned up. He asked us where we were going when these things happened—to heaven or to hell? The sleeves of his black robe waved around as he talked and his face got red under his white hair. I'd hoped to hear about Moses or some other person in the Bible and felt disappointed. I was glad when he finished the story and said a prayer. Then he asked some men to come to the front where each was handed one of the golden plates that I had seen near the front door. I didn't know what to do when one came down my row but guessed you were supposed to pay because people were putting money in them. I didn't have any. I left without talking to anyone and decided there and then that I wouldn't come to that church again. I didn't like such scary stories. I did always remember the picture of Jesus in the beautiful window. It made me feel safe.

CHAPTER 14

A SKIRT TALE

That day was one of those February Sundays when one could justify staying in bed. Michigan winters can be brutal. We had just had a sleet storm followed by a dusting of snow. Nevertheless, I was a girl about to have another adventure on this breath-grabbing cold day.

Having noticed the church as I walked to and from school during the week, I decided to visit on that Sunday. People were gingerly making their way up the flight of concrete steps where the preacher or janitor had already spread sand to prevent worshippers from slipping. I joined the crowd of people wrapped in heavy coats, mittens, and mufflers. A woman in front and to the right caught my attention. Taller than most women I knew and nicely dressed, she greeted people in a friendly manner when suddenly, oblivious to the patch of ice beneath her boots, she slipped and fell. Her Bible landed in one place and her pocketbook in another. People immediately reached out to help her to her feet and to gather up her belongings.

I felt alarmed since I'd never seen an adult fall before and moved quickly toward one of the two doors at either side of the building. There a man in hat and overcoat welcomed me and asked my age. "Eight," I said. He motioned me to come into a large auditorium like the one at school and then pointed to the right where my age group would be meeting for Sunday school. Children were already taking their places on rows of wooden fold-down chair also like the ones at Harding Elementary School. Lively chatter filled the space as I found a place to sit. Within a matter of minutes, the teacher appeared and I was more than a little surprised to see that she was the woman who had fallen on the steps.

I took a deep breath and became alert to any sign that she might not be OK. *She looks fine,* I thought. Relaxing a bit as she placed her Bible and some papers on a small table next to her and welcomed us with a smile, she began.

To this day I have no idea what her prepared lesson was about and I doubt that any of the other children did either. Neither did we know the fall on the steps had popped the button on her skirt, for very soon into her presentation it began to take a trip downward, first off her thin waist, on to her slightly fuller hips, down, past the knees, slowly but surely until gravity had completed its work. While the descent could not have taken long, time seemed to stand still. The renegade skirt lay in gentle folds around her feet and one could almost feel the air being sucked out of the room as together we children gasped. Not a one of us had warned her of the event that had taken place, no raised hands, no faltering voice speaking the words, "Teacher, your skirt is falling down." We had just watched, horrified.

It was what she did next that turned out to be one of the most important lessons I have learned from the *Book of Life*. She pulled the skirt up, held it firmly at the waist and announced, "Children, I have come here today to teach you about the love of God and the devil is trying to keep me from doing it. But, it's not going to work." Then she proceeded with her prepared lesson.

A little leery of visiting the church again, as the drama was a bit much for me, meant I would never learn the teacher's name. Still, I will always be grateful for this unnamed one who taught me about the love of God and the power of carrying on. When having messed up, fallen on my face, or lost my proverbial skirt, inner promptings have come to pull it up and keep on with what God has called me to do.

CHAPTER 15

THE DEVIL, POT ROAST, AND HANDEL

She wore her dark hair in a bun at the nape of her neck and sensible brown Oxfords on her feet. From her head to her toes Mrs. Smith was the picture of propriety. She introduced me to good food and music along with theology I would eventually come to reject.

Our meeting came in 3rd grade when Mrs. Smith was a substitute teacher for Miss Brewer who was recovering from surgery. She seemed ancient but was likely in her late thirties. One thing is for certain, she acted as a rescuer. Though several kids in my class appeared needy, I was the one to receive an invitation to go with her to church and then join her for Sunday dinner. Having yet to meet a teacher unworthy of my adoration, there was little hesitation knowing Momma wouldn't mind. *Yes, yes,* I would like to do this.

The next Sunday morning would be the first of many

church visits with my benefactor. Standing on the front steps of our apartment house, feeling glad to have finished my Cream of Wheat and toast, I waited. A full tummy gave me warmth inside just as my blue coat that Momma had gotten at the Salvation Army kept out the cold November air. I opened my mouth and blew out small puffs of vapor as I waited. Mrs. Smith arrived promptly at 9:30 a.m. as promised.

She drove a black four-door 1942 Plymouth with fuzzy seat upholstery that made it hard to slide across. Mrs. Smith said little as she drove. This was fine with me since the scenery along the way was new. I had never been in this part of town before. We passed several farms and open fields before reaching a gravel road with a white framed house at the end of it. Mrs. Smith announced, "We're here." A small house, not what I expected. Even though it was a nice one it was quite different from the grander church I had visited with the glass picture of Jesus in the boat. That one had high ceilings and lots of beautiful windows that sent colored streaks of light dancing on the heads of people in front of me.

Mrs. Smith parked on a grassy area on one side of the house. Getting out, she greeted a group including two girls about my age and together we walked around to the back door and into a kitchen. Cupboards, a stove and refrigerator, evidence of a family having lived there once, were now a part of a classroom with four or five already seated at a long table. Mrs. Smith was the teacher. More children came in and took their places. I was given a booklet entitled *Weekly Bible Lesson*, in which Mrs. Smith said to write my name as the other children had done. We began on page 6, *A Story of Obedience*. It was about Jesus. As it turned out we heard quite a bit about the devil and hell as well. Mrs. Smith also instructed us on things we should not be doing, like going to movies and reading comic books. Those things were said to be "the devil's playground."

I had no clue as to what such a playground would look like and this idea presented quite a problem to me. I dearly loved the Saturday afternoon matinees with Roy Rogers and his horse Trigger at the Uptown Theater. As for comic books, Captain America was a hero of mine. Yes, the devil likely would not care for these two since they were good guys and thus his enemies. My unspoken question, however, was *Why would they be bad for kids?* As she talked I had a squishy feeling in my stomach like when I ate too much Campbell's tomato soup for lunch. It came back whenever the devil was mentioned. I did feel relieved that she said nothing about listening to the radio, another one of my "vices."

After class and helping Mrs. Smith put things away we moved to the front of the house for church. I tried hard to listen to what the minister said but I kept thinking about the devil on the playground. I was glad when the service was over and we were back in the car for the trip to her house. What a surprise awaited me there. Opening the back door leading to the kitchen I was met with the most delicious aroma. It was the pot roast dinner. After meeting Mr. Smith, who was sitting in the living room reading the *Kalamazoo Gazette*, I felt a little awkward and moved to the kitchen to see if I could help with dinner. The table was already set with matching dishes and a flower right in the middle. It wasn't long before we sat down to eat. The pot roast, potatoes and gravy, along with bright orange slices of cooked carrots, dazzled my taste buds. Seeing the apple pie on the counter top completed a picture of perfection to my young eyes. As expected, it was the best food I had ever tasted. Knowing an offer of help would likely bring smiles, I was happy to show my gratitude by carrying dishes to the sink.

After dinner, Mrs. Smith asked if I would like to go with her to listen to Christmas music. She sang in a chorus that would be rehearsing at Western Michigan College at two o'clock. I was happy to go, expecting to hear familiar carols like *Silent Night* or *Away in a Manger*.

The day had grown bitter cold like so many winter days in Michigan, and as the car slowly heated up I hugged my coat around me waiting for the warmth. Upon arrival at the college we entered a large hall along with others who were finding places on a series of risers. This was in itself a new and interesting sight for me. The director took his place and I took mine on a metal folding chair near the back of the room. Then the music began. It wasn't *Silent Night* or *Away in a Manger,* but *The Glory of the Lord* from Handel's *Messiah.*

I had never heard anything so beautiful. Opening with women's voices, followed by the deep strains of the men's, the music seemed to fill the room and all the space within me as well. Tears began to build behind my eyes until two or three rolled down my cheeks and onto my sweater. Snuffling for lack of a hankie to blow my nose did not interfere with my rapt attention to the music. Mrs. Smith said nothing about my behavior afterward, which wasn't surprising. I sensed she was not a person who was comfortable with such emotional expressions.

I wonder what I would have said if Mrs. Smith had asked me why I cried? How would I have responded? *The music was so beyond my range of experience, so beautiful, it made me cry,* or maybe, *Life at home does not include much beauty. The music cut through the sadness I sometimes felt.* Of course I could not have expressed myself in these terms. I was a little girl with limited vocabulary or practice in finding the right words for beauty and things of the Spirit.

My visits with Mrs. Smith ended at the end of the school year. It wasn't until I reached high school that we met again. She was a sub for an English class. I tried to avoid seeing her, remembering as I did the teachings on hell more than the music of Handel or the pot roast dinners. Had she known I sometimes smoked Lucky

Strike cigarettes and enjoyed talking about sex with my girlfriends, there was little doubt in my mind she would think I was on my way to that fiery place she told us about in Sunday school. She, however, sought me out one day between classes. She had a single message for me before turning and taking her feet, still clad in sensible Oxford shoes, in the opposite direction, "I can tell by your look that you have been going to movies," she said. "You had better watch yourself. They are the work of the devil."

Life is full of unexpected events. Some are pleasant, even grand; others are not. Yet surprises weave their way into our consciousness and bring us joy or doubt, sometimes guilt at not adhering to the "rules." We are often left with questions as we move along on this journey. That being the case, I will always be grateful to Mrs. Smith, who served me wonderful food for the body as well as the soul. As for Mr. George Frederick Handel, *thank you, Sir, for the gift you gave the world, a world including that child who sat on a folding chair in the back of a rehearsal hall.*

CHAPTER 16

THE DAY THE WORLD DIDN'T END

"Katherine, please take your seat." I was in the third-grade and to ignore a request of this nature was not at all like me. Miss Brockway had spoken the words several times that morning because I had left my desk in Room 220 at Harding Elementary at least a half a dozen times. What caused me go to the window and look out across the playground to the heavily-wooded neighborhood beyond? I needed to see if it had begun.

"It" was the fire that was to destroy the world on this day and I was worried. There had been an article in the *Kalamazoo Gazette* about it and that meant it must be true. The article said there were people who had quit their jobs, left their houses or apartments, put on white robes and were waiting on a hill near Western Michigan College. They were going to be picked up there and taken to heaven.

Remembering what the minister said in the first church I visited, the one with the beautiful glass picture of Jesus steering a boat in a storm, caused my fear to increase. He seemed to know all about what was to take place but I wondered if our teachers knew. No one said anything about it on the very day it was supposed to happen.

I had heard something about it the night before. A man and woman who were sitting across from our booth at Kewpies Hamburgers, where we often ate supper, were talking about it. They seemed excited too and talked pretty loud for being in a restaurant.

Momma and Tony listened to their conversation and I could tell Momma felt bad about what they were saying. She wanted to leave as soon as we were finished eating so I didn't get to hear a song on the juke box that night.

I hadn't asked anyone about it except my friend Norma and she didn't know as much as I did. The whole world was going to burn up because God was not happy with us and He was sending Jesus back to take some people He liked to heaven and leave the rest of us here.

Back to the window to see if it had begun. Miss Brockway's voice was now showing signs of irritation.

I wondered what it would feel like to be burned up. I burned my finger one time on the hot plate Momma sometimes cooked on but there weren't flames like when Tony and Momma lit matches to smoke cigarettes. It just turned red and got a blister, then turned kind of gray. I wished I could go to our apartment and be with Momma. I'll bet she was scared and didn't know what to do. I didn't know what to do, but Miss Brockway seemed fine and went on with our arithmetic lesson as if nothing bad was going to happen.

Well, nothing did happen that morning or in the afternoon. Nothing happened when we went on the playground for recess. I kept close watch in the event the fire started and we needed to run. Nothing happened that whole day and I began to breathe a little easier.

I thought a lot about that scary day wondering if the people kept waiting on the hill at Western Michigan College or if they went back to their homes. Had they gotten mixed up about the day the end was supposed to come or did the God just say that in the Bible to scare us? I didn't have an answer but decided I would try not to get so scared if anyone told me that again. I also thought Jesus, who was so good and kind, would probably talk his Father out of doing such an awful thing. What kind of Father would He be to burn us all up?

CHAPTER 17

CHRISTMAS 1943

The State was the finest theater in Kalamazoo. My theater of choice though was the Uptown on the other end of Burdick Street. Kid tickets were 12 cents there whereas the price was 25 at the State. And the Uptown featured Roy Rogers and Gene Autry films, a matter of some importance to me and to Momma as well. First of all money was scarce and, as with me, the two cowboys were her favorite movie stars.

Soon after school had started that fall I had been given a letter by the principle, Miss Honeysett, about a party to be given by the Exchange Club of Kalamazoo. There was also a slip that Momma would have to sign so I could attend. She signed her name, I took it back to school, and a few weeks later got a small envelope with a ticket in it. I brought it home and Momma put it in her jewelry box so it wouldn't get lost.

Now on a cold but snowless December morning before Christmas 1943 I would pass through one of several ornate doors at the State into a world of fun and enchantment without Momma holding my hand. I was eight years old.

There must have been several hundred of us from age six to twelve waiting in a line that snaked from the front of the State, around the corner and down Lovell Street. Momma stood across at Morrison's Jewelry Store and watched until the line moved and we kids entered the theater for the Christmas Party. We all had one thing in common. We were identified as the city's poor for whom the Club put on a grand Christmas Party including gifts, a movie, and a sing-along. Once inside it was *look around as much as possible, stay in line, and watch my step.* I was excited to be there though a little uneasy about the new experience.

I had entered a magical world. The long rows of seats held red velvet cushions, the ceiling looked like the night sky in summer with twinkling stars along with a moon that looked just like the real one. Special box seats ran along each side of the balcony. The whole of the upstairs was empty on this special Saturday. No one had walked up the curving staircase in the lobby because the party would take place on the first floor. It was exactly where we needed to be since that's where the magic began: Soon after I found my seat, a place in the floor opened right in front of the stage and a Wurlitzer organ rose from a lower level in the theater with a man seated on a bench attached to the organ. The music he played could be heard before we even saw him. All the kids stood, rocking from side to side in order to see around the ones in front of them. I had a place in the second row and could see without even stretching.

The only organ I'd ever seen was at the church where the preacher scared me by talking about hell. This one was different. It was grand, beautiful. The music was like nothing I had ever heard before. It vibrated through the theater and felt as if it moved through my body as well. We all clapped and cheered with voices usually used on the playground. The organist then began playing *Santa Claus is Coming to Town* while a large screen dropped down in front of us with the words to the song printed on it along with a ball that seemed to bounce from word to word as we sang along. I stopped clapping and just looked and listened in amazement. It was hard to take it all in.

The music continued for some time until a man dressed in a suit came to a microphone to welcome us and thank all the people and businesses in the city that had helped with the party. Some of the names were familiar like Consumers Power and the *Kalamazoo Gazette*. I often walked past their buildings on my way to school depending on where we lived.

I'm sure we were all told to use our best manners. I know Momma told me to do that but it was hard to sit still and listen knowing some other fun thing would be coming up next. I was not disappointed. After everyone had been thanked and we clapped for them, it was cartoon time. A curtain on the stage opened and behind it was another big screen. Our cheers rang out for each offering, *Popeye*, *Sylvester the Cat*, *Bugs Bunny*, and *Elmer Fudd*. *Mickey Mouse* usually rounded out that part of the program right before an Abbott and Costello film. I had seen two of their movies, "Abbott and Costello Meet Frankenstein" and "Buck Privates" at the Uptown. What a great day being with all the other kids even though I never saw anyone I knew. We were all enjoying the same thing at the same time.

The last part of the program was actually my least favorite. One more curtain on the stage opened and I saw two large Christmas trees one on each side of the stage. Signs beneath them marked one as "Girls" and the other "Boys." There were as many shopping bags on the floor around each tree as there were kids filling the downstairs of the State. Now it was our turn to leave our seats and go up the steps at one side of the stage. We stood, though not very quietly, some shoving the person in front of them a little but then calming down and politely walking up the short flight of stairs.

After receiving our shopping bags and walking across the stage to stairs on the other side we made our way back to our seats to inspect the contents of our bags: a small sack of hard candy, a book, sometimes a game, and a doll. The boy gifts were identical except for the doll. They had a truck or baseball instead. There was also an orange for each of us, something I don't think I ate any other time during the year. Everything had been just grand and I thought about coming again next year if Momma signed the paper and didn't lose the ticket I would bring home. I decided I'd better start reminding her right after the party when she came for me at the magnificent State Theater.

CHAPTER 18

TILLY FRIEDMAN

Webster defines "angel" as "an attendant spirit." Mrs. Friedman was such a being to me, and I may have been one for her, as well. We were present and available to one another.

Her first name was Tilly. As a child in the 1940s, I respectfully called her "Mrs. Friedman" during the short time we lived in her upstairs apartment. She measured less than five feet in height, had wavy black hair, and wore thick-lensed glasses that caused her brown eyes to appear much larger than they were.

Mrs. Friedman and I visited nearly every day after school that fall of 1943. She would ask me about the things I was learning or the movies I saw on Saturday afternoons. Invariably, she would include a request that I sing for her. *Mexicali Rose* was her favorite song, one I often heard Gene Autry sing on the radio. I had memorized the words and was happy she wanted to hear it.

We went into her living room, where she sat down in her favorite chair that matched her maroon Chesterfield couch. On sunny days, the light filtering through lace panels at the windows made shadows dance around our feet. As I began the song, Mrs. Friedman's slight frame swayed a little or she moved her hands as if directing me. The hint of a smile appeared as I sang, but it soon disappeared as the recital ended. Then she removed her glasses, took out an embroidered hanky from her dress pocket on the skirt portion of her dress, and wiped her eyes. I, not knowing what to say, looked around at a wall of pictures to my right, imagining that the people in them, some appearing to be quite old, were part of the audience. Mrs. Friedman thanked me for the song and then reached into the other pocket of her dress, this time to retrieve a nickel she had placed there, payment for my performance. In retrospect that was a pretty good day's pay, since a loaf of bread in 1943 cost nine cents and a quart of milk, twenty-seven cents.

One day I decided to show Mrs. Friedman what I did with my nickels. Entering her kitchen as usual, I held a War Savings Stamp Book in my extended right hand. All the kids in school had them. We pasted stamps received in exchange for the nickels, dimes and quarters that went toward the war effort. I had been able to buy several stamps since beginning my singing career in Mrs.

Friedman's living room. She listened carefully to my explanation and then took out another of her delicately designed hankies, removed her glasses, laying them carefully on the kitchen counter, and wiped her eyes.

"That is a fine thing to do, Katherine," she said in her distinctive accent.

Word was that Mrs. Friedman had left her native Poland in the fall of 1938, soon after Hitler's soldiers invaded the Sudetenland. She fled with her parents while her young husband stayed behind to handle family business affairs before his own exit. He never made it out, and Mrs. Friedman never heard from him again, at least not directly. From other Jews who were able to escape, she learned of the walling off of a portion of Warsaw to create a ghetto and the arrest and imprisonment of the Jews.

War news was not new to me. World War II dominated life in the 1940s. It was always close to thought, whether due to FDR's Fireside Chats, the war ration books, signs with stars placed in windows as indication of a family member serving in the armed forces, victory gardens, or the newsreels at movie theaters.

On most Saturday afternoons, I could be found at the Uptown Theater where, after the cartoon and before the feature, Lowell Thomas's voice would remind us of the horrors taking place in the Far East and Europe. I recall scenes from the uprising in the Warsaw Ghetto in April of 1943. Though they were short clips, they stayed with me. Young men and women serving as untrained, teenaged resistance fighters had surprised the Nazis with homemade petrol bombs and small arms they had smuggled in through the sewer system. The Germans had not expected it. The fighting would go on for 28 days, ending with the complete destruction of the Warsaw Ghetto. Other scenes of Jews being transported to the so-called "labor" camps were shown, as well, Jews with yellow stars sewn to their clothes. The scenes brought on nightmares for me.

I never mentioned the newsreels to Mrs. Friedman the one who was present—my angel, but talked instead about the movies with Roy Rogers, or Gene Autry singing "Mexicali Rose." I missed her when we moved, and I think she may have missed me, too.

Mexicali Rose, I love you. Mexicali Rose, good-bye.

Me at age 9.
Anticipation of making music.

CHAPTER 19

MONDAY MORNING JOY

What I lacked at home was readily available at Harding Elementary School: order, stability, and pure joy. Happiness might strike at any time like the Monday morning in the spring of 1944 when all students began the week in the usual way by stepping through the big double doors of the auditorium and finding a place to sit for assembly. Flipping down the seats in the long rows of wooden chairs, we knew what to expect. Several teachers were on the front row ready to begin the ritual. Following a greeting, Miss Honeysett, the principal, asked us to stand for the Pledge of Allegiance. A gentle rustling sound filled the room as we got to our feet and placed our hands over our hearts, *I pledge allegiance to the flag of the United States of America and to the Republic for which it stands.* I liked saying the pledge while looking at the American flag being carried in by a sixth grade boy. It seemed like a good thing to do. I stood as tall as I could. Miss Miller then took her place at the piano next to the stage and played the introduction to the *Star Spangled Banner*. I sang in my biggest voice even though I still got mixed up on a few words. Next came the announcements.

Miss Miller took the microphone and, after a few crackling sounds her friendly voice filled the room. "Is everyone able to hear me?" With no raised hands to say otherwise she continued. "We will be starting a new program at Harding. I know some of you will want to be a part of it. Students that would like to learn to play a stringed instrument will be able to do so. The school district will supply us with violins, violas, and cellos and those who sign up will meet twice a week in small groups to learn to play the one you choose. If you are interested please come to the music room to sign up and get a paper to take to your parents explaining the program." With that she sat down again. Learn to play an instrument, to make music. I wanted to jump up right then and wave my arms; *I want to, I want to!*

Other announcements followed but I didn't hear them because I was so excited. I could barely sit still on the hard wooden chair. Lucky for me Miss Miller was my homeroom teacher so I would be going straight there after assembly and I would sign the paper. I knew which instrument I wanted to play, the violin. Miss Miller had played a record of violin music by a man named Joseha Heifitz. She said the music was written by J. S. Bach. I had never heard of these people but the music was so beautiful, so perfect. On that day I thought the violin must be the most wonderful instrument in the world. And to think I was going to learn how to play one. I felt like getting up and dancing around the room!

We were finally dismissed and I hurried to homeroom to get my name on the list, second in line after my friend Virginia who signed up for cello and followed by Norma Wooden who had come in behind me to sign up for the viola. We would be in a group together. This made me happy because Virginia and Norma were my good friends.

Miss Miller had told us the instruments would be waiting in the music room the very next Monday and that we should plan to stay after school so we could *meet our instruments.* I loved the idea of meeting my violin. I thought about the violin all week and wasted no time in getting to the music room when the big day finally arrived.

As Miss Miller called our names we were to come forward, pick up our instruments and move to one of the long tables in the back of the room. Laying the case down and opening the two clasps I carefully lifted the lid. What a beautiful sight, a shiny, reddish-brown violin. Miss Miller came to each of us showing us the correct way to pick up our instruments with one hand on the neck and the other at the bottom. That, of course, did not include cellos. She then pointed out the four strings, the bridge and tuning pegs, and the two *f*-shaped openings that let the sound come out. After that we all put our instruments back in their cases and took out the bow that had its special spot under the lid of the case. We learned that the soft white part hooked to the wooden section was made of horse hair. I was amazed. *Who ever thought of that?* I wondered. A small oblong shaped box held rosin for the bow. Miss Miller told us to study and learn the parts of the violin that were described in the music book she then handed out. We should, however, wait to play it until we met on Wednesday. I was so ready to learn. Feeling happier than I could ever remember being and proud to be carrying something as important as a violin, I left for home that day.

Once in the front door of the apartment house on Burdick Street where we had recently moved, I told Momma to come see the violin. Putting it on the kitchen table and after waiting for her to put out the cigarette she was smoking I pointed out all the parts Miss Miller had described, all I could remember that is. Momma seemed pretty interested but didn't ask any questions. I closed the case and carried it to the daybed where I slept, sliding it underneath where it would be safe. I would look at the book Miss Miller gave us, after I found something to satisfy my growling stomach.

My love for the violin grew in my years at Harding Elementary as did my happiness over being in the trio Virginia, Norma and I created. I thought we sounded wonderful and I guess Miss Miller did as well because once in fifth grade she arranged for us to go to play on

WKZO radio upstairs in the State Theater building.

On the day of the program we entered a small room different from any I had seen with a microphone hanging in front of where we would sit and across from it a slanted table with knobs and switches. The announcer had what looked like little ear muffs over his ears when he explained that a sign on the wall with the words *On the Air* would turn red when it was time for us to begin. He would introduce the show and Miss Miller would tell us when to start playing.

There was a radio in the place we lived then and I told Momma to be sure to listen at 2:00 p.m. for the program. She did and she said we sounded really good; she liked when she heard the announcer read my name along with Norma's and Virginia's. I felt so proud and happy about being on the radio even though my bow accidentally touched the microphone when I raised it to play. No one said anything about it and neither did I. Momma said she hadn't heard it.

That year Miss Miller took me to Western Michigan College to play my violin for a man who was a teacher there, Julius Stulberg. The piece I played was a mazurka that I knew by heart. He talked with Miss Miller afterward. I didn't hear all they said but Miss Miller told me he thought I had promise and should be in the Junior Symphony. I told Momma when I got home. She said she didn't know anything about symphonies.

CHAPTER 20

A SCARY MONDAY MORNING

Could it actually be spring or was the beauty of this April morning just a teaser with more snow and cold still to come. Feeling happy to be off to school, as was usually the case, I breathed in the fragrance of my favorite flower, the lilac, already in bloom in many yards on Maple Street. My thoughts then turned to my birthday a few weeks away. Yesterday I had told my new friend, Helen, that I would soon be nine and she asked me what size dress I wore. "I'll tell my mother I want to give you a new dress for your birthday," she said. *Suppose she meant it?* I wondered. Thinking over the conversation as I walked, I lingered on the idea of having a new dress to wear, wondering what color it might be.

Best forget about the dress and pay attention to where I was placing my feet. "Step on a crack and break your mother's back," was the saying. Knowing it couldn't be, still I didn't like the thought of breaking Momma's back. Just looking down occasionally allowed me to see the beautiful trees wearing fat buds and a robin scratching for its breakfast. The moist ground would be sprouting grass in a few weeks, rich green and good to walk on barefoot.

"Little girl," came a voice from behind me. "Little girl, I have some candy. Would you like some?"

What? I thought, turning to see the tall man who lived on Dutton Street near our new apartment. I didn't know his name but had seen him a few nights before sitting on the front porch with a man and woman I thought must be parents.

"Come with me for a minute and I will give you some candy. It's just behind the house here. Come on now, you won't be late for school."

A thought came to me, *Get away. Don't talk to him. Just keep walking.* The breakfast I had eaten no longer felt good in my stomach. *Don't talk to him.* I had heard the story of Adam and Eve once when I visited church with Mrs. Smith and thought it would have been better if Eve had never talked to the snake. She should have run away from the snake or at least walked away fast just like I was doing. Picking up my pace now, afraid he was catching up with me and would grab me, I forgot all about watching for cracks in the sidewalk. My legs felt wobbly so I decided not to run but needed to know if he was still there. I turned to look. He was still there. I didn't have the word for what he was doing then. I learned the term *exhibitionist* years later. In that moment I was just scared. He said nothing, only stared at me.

Picking up my pace to a near run now I turned on Rose Street where, to my relief, cars were moving in both directions. Surely he wouldn't show himself for all the drivers to see. Going to the crosswalk and waiting for an opening in traffic I crossed to the other side. No more looking back just hurrying on, shaking inside but starting to breathe easier, wondering about a different way to go home after school.

I decided not to tell anyone about what had happened. What words would I use? I swallowed the tears coming into my throat. What if I told Miss Miller and she thought I had done something wrong? She was my favorite teacher and I wanted her to keep liking me. No, I wouldn't tell her. I couldn't tell Momma. What would she do? Yell, get mad? No, I wouldn't tell anyone. There was no help that Monday morning except for the thoughts that told me to get away. *Could they have been angel thoughts like people in the Bible heard sometimes?* I wasn't sure but I was glad for them.

School was different that day. Soon after I arrived all of us, students and teachers alike, went into the auditorium for the assembly as we always did on Monday morning. I didn't say the Pledge of Allegiance in a big voice this time. My mouth moved but I didn't hear words coming out. Once I felt like crying and had to bite my bottom lip to keep the tears in. There were so many people in the big room and yet I felt all alone.

After the announcement we all went to our homerooms where I slid into my desk and reached down to get the book from beneath the seat. I had already read *The Boxcar Children* twice. I looked through the pages at drawings of the four children who had no parents to take care of them and lived together in a train boxcar. They knew they had a grandfather somewhere but believed he was a cruel man and did not want him to find them. What fascinated me about the book was the way the children took care of themselves by finding things from a town dump like spoons, plates, a kettle, and even a chipped cup for the youngest boy named Benny. The older boy went into town where people paid him to do work in their gardens. He used the money to buy meat, bread, and milk for the children. Big sister, Jessie, prepared what he brought back to the boxcar. They found wild berries to eat as well. Thinking about them made me wish I had brothers and sisters who I could be with and talk to when I felt bad. I knew a big sister like Jessie would put her arm around me and say she was sorry the man had frightened me on the way to school earlier that morning. She might even say I had done the right thing when I hurried to get away from him. Sometimes when I felt afraid and didn't know what to do I would think about Jessie and wonder what she would do.

I didn't feel as lonely after looking at the pictures in the book. I liked the story as much as the Moses story in The Bible. God had helped people in both of them. I guessed He must be helping me as well.

CHAPTER 21

THE SPA HOTEL

We moved a lot when I was young. I didn't mind. It was just what we did. I was usually happy if the place was free of bugs and had a radio so I could hear my favorite programs, *The Lone Ranger*, *Let's Pretend* and *Lux Radio Theater*. The Spa Hotel had bedbugs and no radio. It was the worst place we had ever lived. Thankfully, we were only there for about three months.

An electric sign hung over the front door with little red lights spelling out the words *Spa Hotel* and *No Vacancy*. The "No" could be turned off if rooms were available. I did like the sign. We had never lived in a place with a blinking, red sign before, and I thought it quite nice.

The door leading to the vestibule was hard for me to open. It was heavy and on school days it meant laying my violin case on the sidewalk, dragging the door open while gripping my books, then holding the door with my body and retrieving the precious instrument. It was quite a feat for a nine year old during the winter months we lived there. The frosty air stayed trapped in the vestibule foyer as I'd make my way to the lobby on the second floor.

Light bulbs hanging from long electric cords along the stairway made odd shaped shadows on the walls. Going up the stairs I counted each one—*fourteen, fifteen, sixteen*. I did not like moving away from the fresh outdoor air to the unpleasant smell of stale cigarette smoke and urine rising from the stained carpet. The load I was carrying also kept me from moving as quickly as I would have liked.

Maxine, the woman sitting behind the desk to the right of the stairs, always looked tired, with dark circles under her eyes that gave her a ghostly look. She sat on a high-backed stool with her face resting on one hand and her elbow on the counter. Flipping the pages of a movie magazine, she only glanced my way. I said nothing to her but a quick look to my right into the sitting area let me know if anyone was sitting on a couch or in one of the overstuffed chairs. A few men, too old to go off to war, usually occupied them. I never went into the space. No one told me to stay out, but there was nothing in the room of interest except perhaps the steam radiators lining one wall. Their *rattle, rattle, hisssss* produced an appealing rhythm.

The room we stayed in was the first one on the right

past the lobby. It was long and narrow with two beds, one against the wall in the middle of the room and a smaller one, which was mine, on the outside wall. Faded brown chenille bedspreads covered each bed. On a small table next to Momma and Tony's bed was a hot plate Momma used to heat soups or make scrambled eggs.

Two chairs and a larger table near the window, my favorite place to do homework, were now occupied by Momma and her friend Joyce Reynolds. Joyce had red hair the color of the blinking lights on the hotel sign. I didn't like her. She insisted on talking to me as if I were a baby and would ask me to sit on her lap, not once, but three or four times whenever she visited.

Ridding myself of my winter coat and boots as I said hi to Momma, I decided to look at the book I had checked out from the school library. I had wanted to practice on my violin but was not too keen on doing so with Joyce Reynolds in the room. Instead I opened a small cupboard door, took out two Dutch Windmill cookies and sat on my bed to concentrate on the story while Momma and Joyce talked.

Something didn't feel right to me and when I looked up I knew why, Joyce was watching me. "Why don't you come here and sit on my lap?" she asked. I shook my head to say no, Momma sat there and said nothing and Joyce changed her position in the chair spreading her legs apart. She wasn't wearing underwear. I felt an anxious feeling that often came when I didn't understand something. I wondered what I could do to make the feeling go away. Then an idea came to me. I quickly closed my book and announced, "I'm going to practice my violin now."

It did not take long for Joyce Reynolds to put on her coat and scarf and say good-bye. My plan had worked!

I was so mad at Momma. I wanted to shout at her for having this person here. What is the matter with her? What is wrong with Joyce Reynolds? The women I admired would never keep asking a big girl like me to sit on their lap and, on top of that, not wear underwear. My teachers wouldn't, neither would Eleanor Roosevelt, or Dale Evans who was Roy Roger's girlfriend in the movies. *Why does Momma let her come here? I will never be like Joyce Reynolds,* I thought.

When Tony came home we bundled up for our walk to Kewpies for a hamburger, something we did most nights. I was particularly happy to be out in the fresh, winter air. It helped me forget Joyce Reynolds.

While we lived at the Spa something happened to a girl named Dolly who lived across the street at the Arcadia Hotel. She was a grade ahead of me at school and her parents managed the Arcadia.

Dolly looked older than the rest of the girls her age, and she acted older, too. She never played with us on the playground unless the teacher told us to pick teams for softball or relay races.

One day things seemed different when I arrived at school. Something was wrong, and I had no idea what it might be. There was a tingling on the top of my head as well as a knot in my stomach. Soon I discovered the cause of my discomfort—something had happened to Dolly. A man who stayed at the Arcadia Hotel had raped her. I wasn't sure what that meant but I did understand that she was hurt and her parents had taken her to Bronson Hospital, just across from Harding Elementary.

Our teachers told us to stop talking in class several times that day, but none of them offered an explanation about what had happened to Dolly.

I was able to get information from my friend Norma. Her mother answered the question of what happened to Dolly and, in fact, explained all sorts of things to Norma, including the meaning of words we saw scrawled on the side of the *Kalamazoo Gazette* building. I could not imagine Momma talking about those things. She wouldn't know what to say. I was happy that Norma was my friend, but I didn't say anything to her about Momma's friend Joyce Reynolds.

Dolly came back to school in a few days, and we all watched her to see if she was different. She was, in a way. She smiled when I looked at her and flipped her shoulder-length hair as if she were special. I didn't ask her any questions since she wasn't my friend, but I noticed she seemed to like the attention she was getting.

Now even more watchful of the men who stayed at the Spa, I hurried past any on the stairs and continued to scan the lobby without making eye contact with those who were sitting or lying there.

A thought came to me: *I should always carry my violin with me, and if anyone bothers me, play it. Maybe they will decide to go away like Joyce Reynolds did.*

It was a happy day when we moved to another apartment, one with more than one room and a bathroom that was not down the hall. I did think about Dolly for a long time, though. I thought about Momma, too, and why she did not say anything when Joyce Reynolds kept asking me to sit on her lap. I had told her I didn't like it.

When I was older I began to think Momma didn't have very much to do just like me in the summer when school was out. She didn't have a house to take care of and she didn't cook and bake like Emma and other mothers I knew. She did go with Emma to clean people's houses, but not very often. I believe Joyce Reynolds kept her from being so lonely.

CHAPTER 22

FINDING MY VOICE

Three gentle taps on the door, a sound I recognized even before Miss Miller rose from the piano bench to attend to the interruption. I knew it was Momma. It had happened enough times during music class for me to dread the tentative knocks that announced her presence. A feeling of dread came over me as my favorite teacher opened the door, looked my way and gave a nod, signaling me to come. It was the fall of fifth grade.

Why did Momma do this? Other mothers didn't come to school except for when they were invited to special programs. I felt embarrassed and could feel my face getting hot the way it did when I had a fever. I had asked Momma not to do this, but here she was again in my favorite place in the whole world. I loved school and especially this room with the piano and the pictures of Mozart and Beethoven and the blackboards with their trays of white chalk and rectangular erasers that fit perfectly in my hand. I was glad when it was my turn to clean them of the dusty, white build-up of chalk. I practiced making patterns as I pounded them on the designated wall outside. School was my place. I didn't think about Momma when I was here and that felt good. But today she had come again.

Momma looked nice enough standing there in the second floor hall wearing her favorite dress with the small, red roses on the material, her hair combed up on either side and hanging down in the back. It reminded me of Joan Crawford in a movie I saw at the Uptown Theater. Still, it was hard to smile at her since I was not happy about her being there.

"What, Momma? What do you want?" I asked in a whisper to make sure my classmates could not hear, even though I had closed the door. She knew the routine and whispered back to me.

"I wanted to tell you I might not be home when you get out of school. I'm going to my lady friend's house. Do you remember Dorothy? She lives on Walnut Street at the corner of Vine. Just go home after school, and if I am not there, I will come soon. The key is under the mat."

"OK, Momma. I will. Now go, because I have to go back to my music class. I'll see you later."

After making sure Momma was on her way, I opened the door, walked quickly to my desk and slid into the seat. Miss Miller was talking about the song we were learning and did not look my way. She was the only one who didn't. Alfred Pearson put his hand over his mouth, and I knew he was laughing by the way his head was bobbing up and down. I might laugh, too, if Alfred's mother came to school like mine did. I so wished she would stop. Even though I felt nervous, I liked singing Brahms's *Lullaby*. It helped me feel better.

As the bell rang, signaling the end of school, Mrs. Hatton the office secretary walked hurriedly into the room and spoke to Miss Miller. I couldn't hear what she told her, but I soon found out.

"Katherine, Miss Honeysett would like to see you in her office."

Our principal was quite large and had a big voice to match her size. It wasn't at all like Miss Miller's gentle tones, which sounded like a song when she spoke. Miss Honeysett was kind of scary, but sometimes she said nice things and smiled when she talked. One Monday morning in assembly she told us all about seeing a student walk to school that morning so interested in the book she was reading, she did not see her drive past. Then I heard her say my name. It was me she was talking about. I liked that she did that. Now, as I followed the secretary to the office, I had a feeling that today she wouldn't be saying anything nice.

Her office was pleasant with two windows looking out at the big maple tree in front of the school where the crossing guard stood. Now I wished I was out crossing the street rather than looking at her from across the big wooden desk. Miss Honeysett began.

"Katherine, I saw your mother at school again today. What did she want?"

Worried because she wanted to talk about Momma, and feeling shaky inside, I answered her question, keeping my voice steady, wondering what she would say next. She cleared her throat and picked up a pencil, tapping the point on the desk two or three times before she spoke again.

"Katherine, you are living closer to Lincoln School than you are to Harding and I have decided you will need to go there." Our last move had been outside Harding Elementary's boundaries. "We cannot have your mother coming to school like this anymore. I tried to explain this to her some time ago, but she doesn't seem to understand. Tell her when you get home that you will need to change schools."

I was shocked. My face felt like it was on fire, and I thought I would cry. Go to another school and not see Miss Miller or my other teachers or be with my friends? Lincoln was a school for colored kids, as everyone called them, and I was sure I would be the only white person there. (A note to any who think segregation did not exist in the north…it did. We just said colored people liked to live together in the same neighborhoods and, of course, those neighborhoods were poor ones, as were their schools.)

The dam broke as I got up to leave, and, with tears streaming down my face, I made my way back to Miss Miller's music room.

Please let her be there, I said to myself, as she came out into the hall then stopped short when she recognized my distress.

"Katherine, what is it child?"

I did my best to report what had happened between, what were by then, deep sobs.

Suddenly she looked different. Her brown eyes were not as happy as usual and her voice was different, too. She sounded a little like Miss Honeysett.

"You go in my room and wait for me. I'll be right back."

With that she turned in the direction of Miss Honeysett's office. I went into the classroom and waited, still crying and trying to catch my breath. It seemed like a long time before I saw her come through the door and walk toward me.

She wiped my face with a wet cloth she had brought with her and said I could stop crying, everything was alright.

"You don't have to go to another school. Tell your mother she must stop coming to school. It will be OK. I will write a letter for you to give her, explaining why she should not come anymore. You can read it to her. I know she will understand."

Feeling calmer as she talked, I hoped she was right. Momma didn't understand some things. I would have to help her understand.

Momma was home when I got there, and I began to yell at her, something I had not done before. Momma yelled at me a lot, and now I was doing it.

"Stop coming to school. If you come again, I will have to go to Lincoln School. I don't want to go there. I want to stay at Harding Elementary."

The angry feelings began to lessen as my energy went into the words and the volume of my voice. It had an effect on Momma. She looked scared.

"I won't come to school again. I promise." Now her voice was shaky the way mine had been when I was with Miss Honeysett.

Feelings of triumph were mingled with sadness over yelling at Momma and scaring her as I did. I wanted to cry again, too.

The trauma of that childhood moment led me to a discovery: What I said *could* make a difference. The words and the way they were used *mattered*. In fact, I could make them work for me. Realizing for the first time how important words could be, I knew instinctively I would make use of this newly discovered ability in the future. I did not like the yelling and decided not to do that again. This was not the case, however. Momma and I yelled at each other a lot in the years ahead, adding guilt to the weight of the anger I felt toward her.

At the time of this incident, it seemed clear that something just wasn't right with Momma. I wasn't sure what it was except that she was lonely when I was at school. Wishing this were not true but more than anything wanting to stay at Harding Elementary, I realized years later that Momma must have wanted me to go there, too. Why? Because she kept her promise: there were no more taps on the door of the music room. She never again came looking for me, and thankfully, it wasn't long before we moved to an apartment in the Harding Elementary School district. Momma had understood me.

CHAPTER 23

DIFFICULT TIMES

It was summer 1945. No one knew I was depressed, least of all me. I'd never heard the term and I doubt anyone even thought about childhood depression then.

President Roosevelt had died in April, increasing my sense of foreboding and making me wonder what we would do without him. I missed hearing him on the radio, his voice so reassuring and kind, but remembered what he said about fear being all we had to fear. People in Kalamazoo came out in the streets on the day of his funeral, as if the train carrying his casket might pass through. I think we just wanted to be together.

I felt sad or afraid much of the time and wished I were in school since there was little to do that interested me throughout the long summer days. To add to my woes we now lived miles away from the library. It was too far to walk, which meant my reading materials consisted of old comic books. Plus, Momma and Tony were mad at Grandpa about something and so we were not taking the bus to Gourdneck Lake either. Emma and Grandpa lived right next to the lake and I was never bored there. I fished with my cousin Charlene who lived across the road and loved my walks in the near-by woods.

Thoughts about our country's safety after the president died were not the only ones that troubled me in the summer of '45. I had pin worms. I thought they would probably eat me up from the inside out. We kids had a song about such an event:

"The worms crawl in, the worms crawl out.
They turn our innards to sauerkraut."

I never told anyone about the pin worms. It was too embarrassing.

As if life without FDR plus the invasion of pin worms were not enough, there was confusion about sex. I had questions but didn't feel safe asking anyone around me, especially Momma. She wouldn't know how to handle them; I was sure of that.

One night while babysitting for the Murphys who lived downstairs and taking their suggestion to spend the night since they would be coming in late, I fell asleep on their overstuffed couch. The sounds of sex awakened me. I could see the clock on the bookcase: 2 a.m.

As with Momma and Tony, who made similar sounds in the night, the Murphys seemed to be enjoying themselves. I remembered when I had once recruited

Billy Lamb to imitate with me what Momma and Tony did. We were both about four. A neighbor, who happened to walk by saw us on the porch, scolded the two of us, and then marched off to report us to our mothers. I made a quick escape into a closet and got behind some long coats. Still, a spanking was forthcoming when Momma found my hiding place, and I wasn't able to play with Billy anymore. Honestly, grown-ups were the strangest things. Why should there be punishment for what I had seen them do?

Now, curled up on the lumpy couch, I lay very still and listened, guessing that Mrs. Murphy would show signs of pregnancy in a few months. She didn't and I didn't understand. Momma never got pregnant either. I thought something must be wrong with her that kept her from having more babies. My friend Norma asked her mother who told her women had babies after they had sex. It was very confusing to me. I would need to ask someone else.

A train track ran along Michigan Avenue in front of Western Michigan College and through the field behind our apartment house. Three times a day a train rumbled past, rattling the dishes in the open cabinet as well as the bones in my body. One day the thought came to me *to see how close I could walk to the tracks when the train was passing,* never finishing the statement, *before I am pulled*

beneath it. I decided to find out.

The evening train to Chicago came through at sunset every day except Sunday. Judging the time to be near, I left my comic book on the porch swing, hurried down the wooden steps and across the field. I climbed the embankment to the tracks when the engine rounded the curve at the Monroe Street crossing. Like a giant Cyclops, black smoke pouring from its steel head, engine shrieking, it roared toward me. Too frightened to watch, I turned my back and continued to walk as the whistle blew and blew, breaking the stillness of the summer night. A quick look over my shoulder, I could see the engineer as he wildly motioned for me to get away. Despite the frantic look on his face with arm flailing out the side door, I walked on until the deafening fury of the engine reached me. Its power propelled me down the embankment. Lying in the cinders I waited for my breathing to calm and my heart to stop pounding. Finally, I stood up, brushed myself off and made my way back to the apartment, my only companions the fire flies out for their nightly ritual. Anchoring my feet firmly on the floor beneath the porch swing and wondering if the shaking would ever quit, I knew one thing for certain. I would never try anything like that again.

We moved again days before school started in the fall of '45 and I was feeling more hopeful. My fear over FDR's death had subsided as I began to see the new president, Harry Truman, in the movie newsreels. It did worry me, however, that he had ordered an atomic bomb dropped on Japan. What if someone did that to us?

In the fall help came on the issues that had troubled me the past summer. Once again enrolled in Harding Elementary, the nurse, Miss Burns, went through the usual routine of weighing, measuring and giving needed shots. She asked each one of us if we ever saw little worms in our poop. *What?* I thought, too startled to answer since this was the first time anyone had asked me about my poop. "Maybe once or twice," I answered. She gave me a paper that told Momma what she would have to do if I saw anymore. She added with a smile, "We don't want those little pests to be taking the vitamins you need to grow up big and strong." I thought to myself, *They won't get much. Momma only knows how to fix a few things, like scrambled eggs, toast, Cream of Wheat, mashed potatoes mixed with hamburger and sometimes pork chops.* I felt better after talking to Miss Burns and supposed the worms wouldn't kill me after all.

As for my questions about sex: My friend Norma continued to funnel them to her mother, who didn't seem to mind anything she asked. Once when Norma and I were walking home from school, we saw the "F" word written on the side of the *Kalamazoo Gazette* building. I reacted with a look of shock but didn't try to explain its meaning when my friend asked me. She said she would ask her mother and she did. I felt sad not to have a mother like hers.

Several years later I would learn that Norma's mother had given us correct information. Junior high classes included one on health. Seventh graders were divided into two groups, one of boys and the other girls. Each group went to its own room and we saw a movie about the human body that explained things like digestion, blood circulation and conception. I took note that women didn't get pregnant every time they had sex, just some of the time. I thought our bodies were amazing.

CHAPTER 24

CHURCH WITH MISS MILLER

Hurrying into Room 14 on the second floor of Harding Elementary, I hung my coat on a hook in the cloak room and hurried to Miss Miller's desk. She looked up and greeted me with her familiar smile and a *good morning*. I was excited to tell her my news.

"Miss Miller, I sang *Fairest Lord Jesus* at church yesterday. I knew all the words and stood up tall to sing the way you taught us to." The hymn was one we had learned at the beginning of the school day and I had come to love it. Miss Miller gave me her full attention and commented on how nice it was that I could sing with the other worshippers.

"What church do you attend, Katherine?"

"Oh, different ones," I responded. "I don't remember the name of the one I went to yesterday. It's a long name that starts with a 'C', across from Bronson Park."

"Was it the Congregational Church?"

"That's it," I answered. The Congregational Church was a big church with stained glass windows. It also had a choir that sat in front and a wonderful organ, though not as grand as the one at the State Theater that I heard at Christmas time. The conversation with Miss Miller drew to a close as classmates entered the room and I went to my desk in the second row.

After the last bell rang that afternoon, while I gathered up my things to go home, Miss Miller came to my desk and returned to the subject of church.

"Does your mother go to church with you, Katherine?"

"No," I replied. "I go alone." A simple up and down movement of her head was followed by a question I loved hearing. "Katherine, I was wondering if you would like to go to church with me. The one I attend is near Bronson Park, kitty corner from the one you attended on Sunday"

"Yes," I quickly responded. "I would like to."

We worked out the details as to the time she would pick me up and bring me back home so I could tell Momma. Miss Miller was always nice to Momma even when she had come to school and interrupted our music classes. I knew she would say I could go with her to church.

The following Sunday I was up bright and early, waiting on the front porch of the Walnut Street apartment house where we had lived on two different occasions. The funny thing about the house was that all the rooms and hallways were painted a purplish color. I think it was called magenta. I guessed the landlady really liked the color or maybe someone just gave her cans of paint they didn't want. I liked the color.

It was a perfect Indian summer day. The air still held the warmth of summer even as the trees had begun to perform their magic. Maple leaves were already becoming a delicate gold.

I was excited about going to this new church, one I had seen many times while visiting Bronson Park but had not been interested in visiting. The four huge pillars in front gave it a look that didn't seem friendly to me and in fact scared me a little. As an eleven-year-old I knew little about architecture to identify the Neo-classical style of the building or know it was a popular one.

In short order Miss Miller's car drove up at the curb and we were on our way to the First Church of Christ, Scientist on Rose Street and climbing the marble stairs to the front doors that were on the second floor level. Others were already making their way through to a wide hallway. Wanting to keep pace with Miss Miller and, at the same time have a look around, I turned my head to the left and looked into a large, high-vaulted room. The morning light streamed through transparent gold-tinted glass in an oval sky light in the ceiling. I stood for a moment remembering the leaves of the maple tree seen earlier that morning. Never having seen a ceiling like it, I thought it quite beautiful. No symbols could be seen in the room: no cross on the wall, no biblical scenes in stained glass like the ones in other churches I had visited, no altar table or candles—only a platform with two upholstered chairs and two lecterns. The only decorations were quotes stenciled on the wall in large brown letters on either side of the platform, one from Jesus and the other, Mary Baker Eddy, the founder of the religion. Directly behind the lecterns, with nothing else to distract from the message were the words, *God is Love*. Everyone entered in silence while the organist played music that was new to me.

Miss Miller led the way down a long flight of marble stairs along with many other adults and children to the first floor where we would have Sunday school. After attending the church for some time, I learned that children did not attend Sunday services upstairs in the room with the beautiful ceiling until they turned eighteen. Looking around the large room we were in with its neatly arranged tables and chairs, I noticed over a platform the same words I had read in the auditorium, *God is Love*. It seemed a good thing to paint on the walls of a church. A man and a woman sat in chairs on either side of a lectern and, after we had sung a song, they took turns reading from *The Bible* and *Science and Health with Key to the Scriptures*, an important book written by Mary Baker Eddy. I soon learned that the church had no ministers like the other churches I had visited. The man and woman were known as Readers.

The Sunday lessons explained that Love is one of the seven names for God, along with Life, Truth, Principle, Mind, Spirit, and Soul. These were capitalized to show they are more than just names, they were God. Many of the Sunday school lessons were difficult for an eleven year-old to understand. This, however, did not keep me from feeling the sweetness of the people.

What I experienced at the Christian Science Church after graduating from Harding Elementary and entering junior high helped me with the transition. Hearing each Sunday that God was Love and that I was God's child was a comforting thought especially when loneliness seemed my closest companion or I had trouble understanding things during some hard days that lie ahead.

CHAPTER 25

A LONG STAY

It was the first time we had lived in one place for an entire school year. Art VanderOover, who had known Tony in the Netherlands when they were both boys made this possible by giving Tony steady work from October to June. Art and his wife Jeannette owned a large tract of land north of town where he grew celery or pansies, depending on the season, while Jeannette managed their small flower shop. The VanderOovers were gracious people. I loved visiting them and feeling free to walk in the straight rows alongside green-leafed celery or in the greenhouses filled with hundreds of flats of multi-colored pansies. The fragrance of the flowers will never be forgotten.

Our apartment that year of seventh grade was located in the basement of Donna and Joe DeLoria's home on

Clinton Street. They had come to the United States from Italy in the 1930s, opened a barbershop and done a good business cutting hair and shaving faces. I had never heard of a woman barber before Donna. The DeLorias spoke to each other in Italian and seemed to enjoy being together. They also owned a lake cottage where they spent their weekends.

A fresh coat of paint and lots of light coming through the high basement windows made our space quite pleasant. I could see Joe's and Donna's feet whenever they walked to and from the garage at the end of the driveway. Joe always led the way. In the winter, snowdrifts hid the view, and Joe was out early with a snow shovel to clear the sidewalk. The same windows framed lilac bushes in the spring. One thing, however, was lacking, the furnishings did not include a radio.

What would I do? The radio had been a source of entertainment as well as a way to escape loneliness. So, when Donna told me I could come upstairs and listen to the stand-up Philco on weekends while they were at the lake, I was thrilled. She always closed the heavy maroon drapes in the living room before she left, and I found the dark, quiet setting just right for the intrigues of *The Green Hornet, Lux Radio Theater, The FBI in Peace and War, The Shadow, Inner Sanctum* and a new discovery, *The Greatest Story Ever Told*, which soon became my favorite. I could hardly wait until the hands on the mantle clock reached 4 p.m. each Sunday and the programs began.

Live actors played the roles of New Testament characters, including Jesus, who was, of course, the star of the show. Before hearing his words, listeners were always alerted by harp music that I thought quite heavenly. Before the show began I got very still, breathing softly, listening to the gentle ticking of the clock or an occasional car passing by on Clinton Street. Since I was still attending the Christian Science Sunday school with Miss Miller and learning more about the man Jesus, I was delighted to occasionally hear a story I had heard at church. The actor playing his part had a wonderfully kind voice, just as I imagined Jesus having. My love for the one called *God's Son* was growing.

A few stories from the Bible were familiar ones that people seemed to know whether they went to church or not, like the one about the first humans, Adam and Eve. It had found a place in my young mind since first hearing it, causing me some anxiety. In it God was a punishing God who sent Adam and Eve out of the beautiful garden because of their disobedience. I had done many things that were wrong, sometimes on purpose and at other times by accident. Would God punish me like he did Adam and Eve? These thoughts often came to mind before I went to sleep at night, and I would change the subject and think instead about Jesus and the stories I knew about him. It was the beginning of my theological wonderings. One thing I felt sure about: I liked Jesus a lot more than I did his Father.

I listened to the radio every weekend until spring,

when another surprise came my way.

Saying good-bye to Harding Elementary School included a consequence I had dreaded: I had to leave my violin behind. It didn't belong to me; it was part of the music program and would be assigned to another student after me. It had amazed me that I could identify musical notes, find them with my fingers on the fret board and create music that sounded quite beautiful, I thought. I seemed like I'd lost a part of me the day I returned it.

One Sunday on our way to church, Miss Miller asked if I missed playing and taking lessons. I answered without having to think: Yes, I did. Then Miss Miller told me of a conversation she had had with a woman named Helene Carmen.

Mrs. Carmen was the first chair violinist in the Kalamazoo Symphony. What a surprise it was to learn she lived a short distance from Joe and Donna's house and our basement apartment. An even bigger surprise came when Miss Miller asked if I would like to babysit with Mrs. Carmen's little girl while her mother gave violin lessons on Saturdays. In exchange, I would receive lessons and the loan of a violin. I jumped at the chance. Mary Lynn, her toddler, was just what this lonely seventh-grader needed, and I was thrilled to be playing the fiddle again with Mrs. Carmen as my teacher. Since the Uptown Theater was on the other end of town, I had not been going to the movies on Saturday and babysitting would give me something to look forward to.

The best part was that I could make music again. Alleluia.

CHAPTER 26

DANCING MY WAY
THROUGH SEVENTH GRADE

The stay in Donna and Joe's basement apartment meant I would be a seventh grader at nearby Washington Junior High School for the entire year. While Harding Elementary was a place of security and warm relationships, my new school would be just the opposite.

The building was old. Its dark wood floors creaked and groaned beneath my feet. The place smelled of old books, years of chalk, eraser build-up and teenagers. It was not an inviting place and, in fact, gave me a nervous feeling as I walked in that first day. I couldn't know I was entering the realm of "mean girls."

Being the new kid because we had moved to a different neighborhood meant none of my friends from Harding Elementary were enrolled in this junior high. As I walked down the 2nd floor hall, searching for my homeroom, I felt as alone as I could ever remember feeling. The buzz of conversations, of which I was not a part, brought me close to tears.

A cute, well-dressed blonde stood with a group of other girls outside Room 21, the homeroom listed on my class schedule. Their chatting and laughing made me wish I were back at Harding doing the same thing with my old friends. All eyes turned toward me. I smiled feebly and said *Hi* before going into the room and finding a desk at the back.

The teacher, Mr. Woods, called roll and I learned that the cute classmate was Juanita Getz. "Skeeter, for short," she announced. She was a leader, the person in charge of the other girls in the class, and she made quick work of letting me know it. The word was out by lunchtime: *Don't talk to the new girl.* It was, however, their duty to whisper comments loud enough for me to hear, opinions about my clothes, hair, and lack of friends. To this they added pushes and shoves when they passed me in the hall. I was totally surprised by their actions. At Harding Elementary I considered all the girls in our class my friends—Norma, Ethel, Virginia, Margaret. *What had I done? Why were these girls acting this way?* I asked myself.

Since I was learning about prayer at the Christian Science Church, I began to talk to God many times a day. *Please God, make them like me.* But, despite my prayers, the bullying continued and my sadness grew day by day. *Was God listening?*

Lunch in the school cafeteria had become a solitary experience for me until one Monday in late October. The principal announced that a jukebox had been installed in the gym, and anyone who wanted to could go dance or just listen to the music. I was one of the first to come through the door. I loved music, and being able to simply push the button and hear the Harmonicats sing, *Peg O' My Heart* or Vaughn Monroe croon *Ballerina* was going to be a huge treat.

While going over the selection of songs, Bill Moore, a boy from my homeroom stepped up to the jukebox. I had noticed him because he seemed friendly and was kind of cute in his horn-rimmed glasses and dark curly hair. *How unfair*, I thought, for a boy to have such curls when my hair was as straight as string. His clothes were nicely pressed and his brown and white saddle shoes always looked brand new.

"Hi. We're in the same homeroom, aren't we? Mr. Woods?"

"Yes," I answered, surprised at being the recipient of his easy smile.

We talked about the songs we wanted to hear and pushed the right numbers when he suddenly asked if I'd like to dance. *What*, I thought. *Was he kidding*?

"I don't know how to dance," I replied. That was not exactly true since I danced polka and the waltz at Finnish parties. If I'd been honest I'd have said, *I would be scared to death to dance with you or anyone.*

"It's easy," he assured me. "Come on, I'll show you."

The room was already filled with the sound of Glenn Miller's *In the Mood* as Bill took his place next to me and became my dance instructor for the jitterbug, showing me what to do with my feet. He was right. It was easy. I forgot the gang of mean girls and sent my heavy feelings through my dancing feet into the gym floor.

It would become the first of many dance dates that continued through the remainder of the school year. Soon I was thinking less about Harding Elementary and letting go of anxious feelings about Skeeter and her gang. As a result, they lost interest in their power game.

It would be many years before I read Margaret Atwood's novel *Cat's Eye,* a story about a young girl who is bullied by one of her peers. The tale took me back to the nightmarish pain of being shunned at Washington Junior High. In Atwood's story the protagonist is so deeply scarred by the abuse that she becomes cold and cut-off from her feelings. For me, I began to wonder if God cared about my problems. An answer had come that was different from my request to be accepted by the girls—one I did not recognize at the time. It became apparent years later when I heard a Native American saying, *When there is spirit loss one must dance their way back to life.* That is what I did in seventh grade. Thank you God and thank you, Bill Moore, wherever you are.

CHAPTER 27

BACK IN THE COTTAGE AGAIN

The *alikempa,* a Finnish term for "little cottage," had been our home several times during my childhood. Grandpa had built it years before on land down the hill from the big house where he and Emma still lived and where Momma had grown up. The reasons for moving back to it were always the same: Tony was out of work, and there was no money for rent. Momma would make the request for help and Grandpa couldn't say no.

As for me, I had mixed feelings about being there again that summer before eighth grade, even though Gourdneck Lake had been a happy place on many occasions. Living a few steps from the lake's edge and hearing the gentle bump of the rowboat against the dock Grandpa had built brought back pleasant memories. Having spent countless hours playing on that pier as a little girl, I must have mopped it hundreds of times. I would lower an old mop into the lake, swish it over the wood until the entire surface was wet, and then watch it dry in the warm summer air. Then I'd repeat the process. I can still recall the feeling of accomplishment at being able to change something. Summer nights might include lying on a blanket down by the lake with my cousin, watching for shooting stars in a Milky Way sky or gathering worms for the next day's fishing trip, after luring them out of the ground with a generous yard-watering earlier in the day. These activities were now passé for a budding eighth-grader.

Old enough now to take the rowboat out alone, I would push off the dock early in the morning to fish in the sparkling, clear waters or just row to a favorite spot where there was a good view of the woods. It was during those times that I began to love dragonflies. The delicate aviators seemed to enjoy resting on my fish line, causing me to pay more attention to them than to the bobber signaling a bite. In the afternoon I might go swimming with my cousin Charlene or sit in my favorite tree and read comic books. Often three or four kids who lived down Mandigo Road came to play kick the can in the evenings. Summertime at the lake was fine with me.

The cottage itself was barely adequate. Grandpa had built it into the side of the hill, and the back wall was the earth itself, which Grandpa had covered with heavy canvas. The first time I saw pictures of American pioneers building sod houses on the prairie, the alikempa came to mind.

An old-fashioned hand pump in the kitchen supplied our water, and we had to climb stairs Grandpa had built into the hill right next to the cottage to get to the bathroom. It was just inside a separate entrance to the main house. The sauna, right next to the bathroom was where we also took our weekly baths. An oil space heater warmed the small cottage in the winter, though not very well, since the cottage had been built for summer living.

The most bothersome thing that summer was what went on between Emma and Momma. It was clear they did not care for each other, and their bad feelings seemed to seep into the space around them. I had stopped trying to help Momma feel better when she was upset, since she still was apt to vent her anger at me whenever I did. It was just better to get away if I could, and I often found refuge on the lake or in the nearby woods.

On the short driveway to Emma and Grandpa's house sat four other houses and a small grocery store that faced Portage Road. Mr. and Mrs. Stone owned the store, and provided one of my favorite activities that summer—free outdoor movies. On Friday nights our family gathered with neighbors and vacationers at the Stone's vacant lot across from the grocery. People began parking their cars in the best spots before supper, while the kids spread old blankets or faded chenille bedspreads on the hard ground. No one seemed to mind when the screen, which hung between two oak trees, rippled occasionally in the night air, giving the actors strange shapes. Sometimes the sound system crackled and snapped. It was a great treat just to be there and the movie-goers rewarded the Stones at intermission by walking across Portage Road to purchase soda pop or ice cream cones at their store.

One Friday night I noticed a girl about my age standing near me in line as I waited to select my treat. She was shorter than I, with straight dark hair and blue eyes. We smiled, introduced ourselves, and on the spot decided to sit together for the second half of the film. It didn't take long for the conversation to begin. Her name was Darlene.

"Is this the first time you've come to a movie here?" I asked.

"I came one time last summer too." she responded. "Who is your favorite movie star?"

"Hmm, I think I like June Allyson and Elizabeth Taylor. Did you see "Little Women?" I was enjoying our conversation.

Then an important question: "What grade are you in? I'm going into the eighth."

"Me too," she said. "Do you like to fish? Do you want to come to my house tomorrow?"

My answer came quickly. The prospect of having a girlfriend after the seventh grade experience when Skeeter Getz and her friends had shunned me was exciting. After the movie, we made plans to meet the next day. Darlene owned a new bike and would meet me halfway between our houses at ten o'clock. We then would ride double back to her house. One of us peddled and the other sat on the back fender, which we reversed on the way back to the cottage late in the afternoon.

Darlene and I became fast friends that summer. We spent most days together sprawled on a blanket, reading and talking endlessly about the things that twelve year-olds talk about. I never spoke of the troublesome times when I felt sad or angry with Momma and Tony, though. I was afraid Darlene wouldn't like me if she knew, and I didn't want that to happen. We would both be starting eighth grade at Portage Junior High in September. We made plans to sit together on the bus and do the same at lunchtime. I had a girlfriend and I was happy.

My training as a violinist had come to a final end when we moved back to Gourdneck Lake. Church attendance ended that year as well since Miss Miller lived quite a distance from the lake and it was no longer convenient for her to pick me up on Sunday mornings. I still listened to the *Greatest Story Ever Told* but was giving less thought to God and the stories of the Bible and more to the business of becoming a teenager. That seemed fine to me.

CHAPTER 28

NEW HORIZONS

Summer now officially over, I stood with a small group of neighborhood kids outside Stone's Grocery, waiting for the school bus. It was one of my favorite days of the calendar year, the Tuesday morning after Labor Day. School started today. Indian summer had commenced with a slight change in the air from summer heat to a hint of fall and I was excited to start my new adventure. This would be my first ride on the big yellow vehicle since I had always been able to walk to school in the past. Now as it came into view I wondered if my new friend Darlene would be on board or if I would need to save her a seat. Within moments the squeal of the airbrakes pierced the morning air, the folding doors opened, and I climbed on with the other Junior High and High School aged riders. Once on I looked on both sides of the aisle but saw no sign of Darlene. *OK,* I thought. *I'll sit on the aisle and save the window seat for her.* I took a deep breath, knowing it would be a better year than seventh grade because of my new friend.

In short order she was sitting next to me and, as we chatted about what the first day might be like, we watched each new passenger climb aboard and be greeted by Jonsie, the bus driver. Some faces were familiar to us from the Friday night movies during the summer.

The trip seemed short; Soon we were inside the main entrance of Portage Junior High and checking the homeroom assignment lists. I hoped they wouldn't be assigned alphabetically since Darlene's last name was Brewer and mine was VanDeWouwer. Good news! We were in the same homeroom and, I felt, off to a great start.

The teachers seemed nice enough. I understood the assignments and in a matter of days three other girls— Dorothy, Nancy, and Sandra joined Darlene and me as new friends. The five of us sat together in the lunchroom and met at each other's lockers between classes to share any news, talk about assignments, or comment on the boys we thought were cute.

Sadly, during what otherwise were perfect school days, one unpleasant and recurring issue did arise for me: I talked too much. In fact, I was once told to sit outside the classroom and, even worse, sent to the principal's office. It was strange because I knew I was doing it, but had difficulty being quiet. I felt shamed and embarrassed by my actions, much the way I did by the things Momma said and did sometimes. There had been a similar experience during the past summer when I visited a Girl Scout troop meeting, but I'd never had the problem in school before. Puzzled, I tried my best to correct my behavior.

Glee club helped stem the flow of words that occasionally escaped from my mouth. Gertrude Lindy, our music teacher, impressed her singers with the need for proper diction and breathing. She also said we shouldn't waste our words because words were important and we needed to think about speaking or singing them. What she said made me remember the time I yelled at Momma when I was at Harding Elementary. Words were important then and they still were. I didn't like scaring Momma the way I did and now I had another good reason for not talking so much. I didn't want to waste my words.

Rehearsal for *Stephen Collins Foster and His Music* began after Christmas break. Several singers were assigned solo parts, and I was picked to sing *I Dream of Jeannie with the Light Brown Hair*. It was to be, said Miss Lindy, "a big production with costumes, two different backdrops, and numbers by the full chorus." We practiced for weeks until our show date arrived, a performance for the seventh-graders and any parents who might like to come.

I didn't invite Momma, afraid I would be too nervous if she was there.

You would have thought we were on Broadway. The show went off well, and Miss Lindy was so pleased she immediately began a campaign to perform it for the high school. The date was soon set for late March. As it turned out, it arrived all too soon.

To our surprise the response of both the high school students and their teachers was quite different from that of our first audience. Our performances were different as well. Upon looking out at a packed auditorium, several singers got stage fright and had to begin their numbers again. Most sang with such quivering voices, me included, that we sounded like Alfalfa in the Little Rascals movies. When it was my turn to move to center stage, I hoped, I prayed, for a fire drill or some similar event to call us to any place but there. The worst part, however, was the audience's response. At first there was a barely audible titter. Then it grew. Soon open laughter erupted from students and faculty alike. There we cowered, girls in hoop dresses and big bonnets and boys in suits from another era, all wishing we were dead. Miss Lindy looked mortified.

In the fall, all having been promoted to ninth grade, we had to meet our audience on different terms. Many of us heard the dreaded question, *Weren't you in that Stephen Collins Foster Show last spring?* I always denied the charge or just acted like I didn't understand the question? *What show? When?*

Even though Momma, Tony and I moved from the little cottage down by the lake before cold weather set in, our future rentals would remain on the same bus route until eleventh grade, giving me precious time with my friend Darlene. We didn't talk much about the Stephen Collins Foster show in later years, and over time I even felt a little smile cross my face whenever I heard the song *I Dream of Jeannie with the Light Brown Hair.*

CHAPTER 29

HIGH SCHOOL GOALS

For the most part, high school was great. I made good grades, had a nice circle of friends, including occasional boyfriends, enjoyed being in plays and glee club performances, and was fortunate enough to have part-time jobs that gave me spending money. Along the way, however, there were a few glitches.

For example, on several occasions I skipped school with my pals to enjoy the arrival of spring at Lake Michigan. Four of us—Nancy, Darlene, Dorothy and I—hopped in Nancy's '32 Chevy, with her at the wheel, and off we went for the hour-and-half trip. Our first outing went smoothly and without apparent consequences. The second one, in late May, did not turn out so well. It probably wasn't a good idea to show up at school after a day at the beach just as classes were letting out, but we didn't want to miss tennis practice at 4:00 p.m. Everett

Bekin, our principal, stood out front directing the buses as we drove up. As a result of our escapade, we were all expelled. And that wasn't all. Before we could be readmitted and allowed to take final exams, Principal Bekin said a parent would need to come to school to meet with him. When I heard the terms, I felt a wave of panic. My day enjoying nature would prove costly.

An unspoken goal I had held to was to keep Momma and Tony separated from my life at school and from my friends. The little cottage by the lake and the other places we lived during high school were off-limits to my classmates. Since we did a lot in groups, I usually planned to meet people either in front of Stone's Grocery or where the party was to be held. If I had to bring either Momma or Tony to school to meet with Mr. Bekin and me, my long-held goal would vanish. I chose Momma even though I knew it would be hard for her.

The appointed day arrived, and Momma and I rode to the school with Darlene and her mother. As we made our way through the main entrance to Portage Senior High and up the stairwell to the second floor, I could see kids looking and talking behind their hands. This didn't surprise me and did not hurt as much as what they had already been doing...shunning us. Apparently, teachers had directed this behavior in order to teach any would-be truants a lesson: No skipping school!

The secretary called Momma and me into Mr. Bekin's office first. He rose from his chair and indicated with a somber nod that we were to sit in the two un-cushioned chairs facing his desk. Concern for my own self subsided immediately as I looked at Momma sitting stiffly on the rigid oak surface. She was visibly shaken. I think Mr. Bekin recognized panic when he saw it and kept the meeting mercifully short, speaking of his expectation of his students making better choices than we had made. Momma and I sat in silence. It was during that brief drama that I decided to never again do anything to put her in such a position.

Feeling grateful for the meeting's end, I left the office with Momma, and we walked down the now empty halls and out the front door. We would wait in the car for Darlene and her mother. My plan to keep Momma and Tony in separate compartments of my life had not changed, but I now had an additional reason for fulfilling my goal—the guilt I felt over putting Momma through such an ordeal.

The next year Tony came close to disrupting my plan again. He was working at a celery farm owned by a well-known family in the community who had a daughter in the grade behind me. He had been there only a few months when he stole a piece of farm equipment and sold it. For this he went to jail. I marveled at his stupidity while I trembled inside, fearing the story would get out. Would his daughter hear the tale at the dinner table and put two and two together when she heard the name VanDeWouwer?

Fortunately, the theft of the farm implement and Tony's time in jail did not become a topic of conversation at school. Gradually, my anxiety calmed and I continued to work toward the goal of getting through high school with a minimum of attention paid to my home life.

CHAPTER 30

JOB BENEFITS AT F. W. WOOLWORTH

The time had come. I needed a job to pay for dental work. Due to poor nutrition and never having seen a dentist, the cavities had multiplied along with the fear of someday becoming toothless like Momma and Tony. A Saturday job until summer and then a switch to full time would give me the money to get started on tooth repair. Working up my courage one April day in 1951, I walked through the front door of the F. W. Woolworth Store on Burdick Street in Kalamazoo without a clue about the importance of my action. Soon I was talking with a slightly overweight assistant manager named Harriet Day. She had well coifed hair, deep blue eyes and a ready smile. I felt at ease as we stood in an employee rest area outside her office on the second floor.

After hearing of my desire for part-time work, excluding the dental problem, she hired me on the spot, even though I would not be 16 for another month and did not yet have a Social Security card. Perhaps she picked up something of my desperation or maybe it was my determination to succeed. Training for the job would be held the next Saturday and my earnings after taxes, $4.20 a day. *Thank you, thank you,* was my response to Mrs. Day, words that circled around in my mind as I exited the back door.

After waiting a few weeks to see how the job worked out, the search for a dentist began. Walking into the lobby of the bank building just doors away from Woolworth's and scanning the directory on the wall I found a name followed by the initials DDS that satisfied my search. I stepped on the elevator and rode to the fourth floor accompanied with feelings of anxiety over the meeting about to take place. Would the dentist understand my situation and be willing to help me? I need not have worried. Dr. Dangreman and Mrs. Dangreman, who was his assistant, heard me out and, after examining my teeth, the doctor said several would need to come out as well as a number of others that needed fillings. Despite the lingering embarrassment at having the couple see my teeth, I offered a possible payment plan of ten dollars a month. The offer was accepted. The two new friends must have heard my sigh of relief because of the load that had lifted. Beginning the very next Saturday I spent my lunch hours in the oversized dentist chair for the many weeks it took to complete the drilling, fillings, and pulling of teeth. I will be forever grateful for the kindly Dr. and Mrs. Dangreman. I still have most of those original fillings.

CHAPTER 31

THE CANDY COUNTER
AND MUCH MORE

My work area at Woolworth's turned out to be the candy counter, and that suited me just fine. I was not, under any circumstances, to eat the merchandise while on the job, but I could enjoy small portions of the goodies during breaks. Not wanting more tooth decay my choice of snacks became cashews, salted peanuts, and the other delicacies I was learning to roast. Keeping the bins filled and arranging the best displays behind the sparkling glass fronts gave me a sense of ownership. Soon I noticed a young man who was also an employee.

He was as skinny as a pole, and wore a navy gabardine suit decorated with a narrow maroon tie. He sported horn-rimmed glasses, had dark eyes and even darker hair that he combed in a grand pompadour, popular at that time. The woman who worked with me said he was the floorwalker. He stopped by several times during the day to remove the growing stack of bills in the registers and provide change when we needed it. A bundle of keys on a thin, silver chain hanging from beneath his jacket gave him an air of authority and importance. Learning that he was a college student working his way through Western Michigan College, I was told to call on him if I had a problem of any sort. I often wondered what sort of situation would require his action.

In addition to his looks, what was it that impressed me about this young man, Doug DeGrow? Unlike the men in my life, he wore a suit. Tony didn't own one, and I had only seen pictures of Grandpa looking handsome in his dark version with a vest and stiff creases in the trouser legs. To me, the suit represented respectability.

Doug obviously valued education, and so did I. School had been my safe haven, the place that opened up a different world and the hopes for a good life. I planned to go to college someday, though I couldn't imagine how that would come about. My curiosity piqued, I decided to find out more about him. My co-worker, who seemed to know a lot about everyone, said he not only attended the Methodist Church but sang in the choir. Wow. Even though I was going to a high school dominated by members of the Dutch Reformed Church, where church attendance was expected whatever the age, he went without the urging of parents just as I did. His family lived in another town and he was on his own. Since I was now going to the Congregational Church kitty corner from the Methodist Church he attended, I wondered if we might run into each other some Sunday after service.

Doug was all business during working hours, but one Saturday morning before store opening we arrived at the employee entrance at the same time and decided to go to the record counter and play new releases. Together we heard Johnny Ray's *Little White Cloud That Cried*, Teresa Brewer's *Wheel of Fortune* and hits by Jo Stafford and Kay Starr. These get-togethers became a Saturday ritual that I looked forward to and, I thought, he did as well.

During my second summer on the job, Doug was not around, and word was he was ill with yellow jaundice and recuperating in his hometown of Pigeon, a small village in Michigan's "thumb." When he did not return I thought, *Oh well, it was nice while it lasted*. He was back in the fall, however, and to my surprise asked me for a date. "Sure," I said, thinking to myself, *I can do this*. We set the date but as it approached I developed a bad case of cold feet. *What would I say to him? What in the world was I thinking when I said yes? He was a second year college student and I was still in high school.*

What I did was stand him up. He told me later he was shocked. This had never happened to him before. It would be several years before we finally had that date, not before the most challenging period of my life.

CHAPTER 32

HE HAD RED HAIR

One Saturday afternoon in May, a group of teenagers swept into Woolworth's like a gust of spring air coming off Lake Michigan and headed straight for the candy counter. This was a common occurrence, and I readied myself to fill their order and even participate in a bit of kibitzing. The four of them wasted no time in making selections—a quarter pound of malted milk balls, the same amount of Hershey's kisses, and six chocolate-covered nut clusters. They were clearly enjoying themselves and included me in the fun through the questions they asked.

"Is the candy fresh?"

"Oh yes, everything is very fresh." I said.

"Do you ever give prospective customers a few samples?"

"No, I couldn't do that," I responded with a smile.

"How long have you worked here?"

"A long time," I answered," but I haven't seen any of you in here before."

I guessed they might be from St. Augustine Catholic School or Central High. It turned out they represented both schools and knew no one from the hinterland of Portage.

As I filled the order, one cute boy with red hair and beautiful brown eyes caught my attention. I believed the same was true for him since he made eye contact and lingered behind after his friends left the store. We exchanged names—his was Bob—where we went to school—he was at Central—and then he asked if I worked every Saturday. I responded that I was behind the candy counter every Saturday from nine to five except for breaks and lunch.

"I'll be here next Saturday at five if you'll go have a Coke with me," he said. I agreed but doubted the meeting would take place.

It came as quite a surprise when I saw him at closing time the following Saturday. Delight would be a better description of how I felt, with an ever-so-slight flutter in the heart. I was sure my smile must have told him how happy I was to see him. He agreed to wait in front of the store while I closed my counter and went upstairs to punch out and retrieve my purse from my locker. Then together we walked down Burdick Street toward Holly's Grill. From this first date it seemed we had always known each other, and before long we were boyfriend and girlfriend. He had a quick sense of humor and cared when I was having a hard time at home. He seemed to understand because he too was going through difficulties. It was first love for us both.

At the time, Momma, Tony and I lived on the far north end of Burdick Street in an upstairs apartment with a separate entrance and four good-sized rooms. The land lady was a grandmotherly woman named Bess Barker whose husband had died years before. She was a no-nonsense kind of person and, I believed, picked up on the tension in the family soon after we moved in. She let me know that I was free to come downstairs to her apartment if I ever needed to. I spent many Sunday evenings watching the *Ed Sullivan Show* with her. In addition, the bus line ran down Burdick allowing me to reach work easily.

Bob and I remained a couple through the summer and our junior year, going to the YMCA canteen every Friday night to dance, enjoying movies and taking long walks in Milham Park. We were in love, and I wore his class ring to prove it.

At the beginning of our senior year, a new job opportunity came along. Michigan Bell Telephone sent representatives to Portage High to recruit students for a new training program. Several of us, my friend Darlene included, showed up for the meeting to see what it was all about. It sounded good. If interested we would begin training in October in a management program that included leaving school early three days a week to study and learn the telephone business from the ground up. We would spend time in classroom work at their offices as well as learn how to be telephone operators. After our graduation from Portage, if all parties were happy with the results of our training, we could become full-time employees or part-time ones if going to college. And we would be paid while we trained.

My first thought was that I would likely see less of Bob. The next realization…this was a good opportunity. Darlene, who had also been hired at F. W. Woolworth the previous summer, joined me in signing on the dotted line. We both planned to continue Saturday work at Woolworth's as well.

Saving the money I earned had been a priority for me and soon I was putting a weekly check in the bank along with the few dollars I made at Woolworth's. I had plans for the money. I wanted to get my own place to live as soon as possible. If I could win a scholarship for college, I might even be able to live in a dorm. I had yet to look at the actual cost of dorm life and would soon discover it was far more than I imagined.

The pressure to move away from Momma and Tony grew stronger in the spring leading up to my graduation. Tony began badgering me about the money I earned. *What are you doing with it? You should be helping pay the bills.* I, in turn, was determined to hold on to every cent. He began to be physical, slamming me against a wall or grabbing my arm when I wouldn't cooperate. At such times, Momma would leave the room looking frightened. More than once I had to wear long-sleeved garments to hide bruises and left the house with puffy eyes and a tear-stained face.

Bob was a great support, encouraging me to hold on and not give Tony any of my savings. We talked about our life together after he finished college at Michigan State, where he would go the next fall. It wasn't to be. Momma thought I was seeing too much of him and took it upon herself to call his mother. Bob's parents then gave him an ultimatum and took steps to break up the relationship. They were Jewish and had had a difficult experience when their daughter's involvement with a gentile had resulted in the birth of a child. They told Bob they would not pay for his college if he saw me again and he succumbed to the pressure. I was devastated over the break-up and furious with Momma for what she had done. I tried not to think about what she might have said to Bob's mother. Embarrassment added to my anger was just too much to handle.

Struggling to finish school and maintain my jobs, depression reared its hydra head. I managed to carry on and began praying for a place to live on my own. I hadn't thought much about God in recent days, even though I was still going to the Congregational Church in Bronson Park. Now I found myself praying silently, *Please, God, help me find a place to go. Help me to make it on my own.* One portion of the prayer would soon be answered.

PART III

CHAPTER 33

MOVING OUT AND SLIPPING AWAY

Momma felt bad about my leaving. It was obvious. The challenge now was of setting my own feelings aside, concentrating on the needs of the moment, namely of getting my things into the blue Samsonite suitcase and leaving as quickly as possible. Walking down the steps, struggling with the load, was the hardest thing I had ever done. Momma was close behind.

I couldn't bring myself to look in her eyes. Even though we had begun to talk about my plans to stay with Mrs. Gilbert, it hadn't sunk in for either of us. My insides felt like wet cloth that had been twisted and wrung out until all the moisture was gone. Neither of us cried, though giving way to the tears might have helped our parting. All she said was, "You'll come to visit me, won't you?" "Yes, Momma, yes, I will. I promise." I gave her a hug and walked to the curb where my friend Andrea, a co-worker at Michigan Bell Telephone stood, waiting to give me a ride. Together we hoisted the suitcase into the trunk of the car. Then settling in the front seat, I stifled my tears without looking back until we turned on Inkster Avenue. Momma had already started up the porch stairs from where she had been standing almost statue-like during those final minutes. She didn't see the wave. Tony had not come out to say good-bye, and that was fine with me.

Graduation ceremonies had taken place just the week before along with final arrangements to board with Bethel Gilbert. Her name had been given to me when I applied at Western Michigan College. She was a woman who helped deserving young people who wanted to attend school and I fit the requirements. My status would be a part-time student at Western while continuing my work at the telephone company.

Mrs. Gilbert lived in a fine old home set back from the road on Oakland Drive. Its front circular driveway and the surrounding woodlands reminded me of the manor houses described in Agatha Christie's mysteries. My new bedroom on the front side of the house overlooked the driveway and seemed pleasant enough. It had a unique smell that emanated from the cedar-paneled closet. The room was well-furnished with cornices at the large window overlooking the driveway with a bedspread to match. As nice as it was, I can't say I was excited. It was more like being thrust forward, do or die, make or break this opportunity. *Was coming here to live the right decision?* The poignant feelings over leaving Momma had given way to a kind of numbness. That, along with the darkness that had been my companion for many months felt overwhelming. It seemed to engulf me in the days ahead as well, affecting both my appetite and my ability to sleep. Nothing tasted good, not even the fresh vegetables I would soon be gathering from the garden on the Gilbert estate. I was dropping weight and developing dark circles under my eyes from lack of sleep.

My stay in what seemed an idyllic setting came to an abrupt ending after only a few weeks. Mrs. Gilbert had been called to California to be with a sick friend, and I would be staying with her son and his family, who lived near the Western Michigan College campus.

As the inner gloom sapped my energy and strength, I found it hard to keep up a semblance of normalcy. I had difficulty entering into conversations or keeping eye contact when spoken to by others. These deficiencies did not make me a welcomed boarder with this branch of the Gilbert family where my duties included occasional babysitting with their two young children. I had no illusions. Soon I was packing again, this time for my move to the YWCA. Mr. Gilbert had been direct when he said it was just not working out. In fact, *I* was not "working out." It occurred to me that I had become like Momma. She clearly was not accepted by so many and now, the growing fear *of being like Momma* was coming true. It was a devastating thought.

CHAPTER 34

NEXT STOP

The Y located at one end of Bronson Park was a place I had visited many times. Its spacious lobby with high ceilings had nicer furnishings than were found in most public places. When I was younger Momma and I would occasionally go to the Y on Sunday afternoons, sit in our favorite Queen Anne chairs, and look at the funnies in the *Kalamazoo Gazette*. I would pretend I lived there, never once imagining that one day I would.

My small room turned out to have none of the elegance of the lobby two floors down only a single bed with a metal headboard, a small desk and chair, and a table lamp. I had never felt as alone as I did in that room. Lying on the bed that first day and looking up at the ceiling, the blackness seemed to close in around me. I wondered why God was punishing me or to be honest, was there a God who cared about me? I saw no evidence of such a one and no thought entered my mind to call a human person for help. In reality there were many such people. Miss Miller, who had been so kind when I was younger, would have responded in some way, as would Dr. Malone, a gentle man who helped me once when I was sick. Joan, my supervisor at work, could also have been added to the list of caring people. It did not occur to me to call Emma or Grandpa, my aunt or my uncle either. I certainly would not try to reach Momma or Tony. That door was closed.

After abandoning my plans to begin fall classes and instead continue full-time work at the telephone company, trouble concentrating while at the switchboard commenced. Several mistakes caused my supervisor, Joan, to call me into her office for a talk. Doing my best to act normal along with a promise of a better performance in the future, I left shaken and feeling weak. If honest I might have told her of the suicidal thoughts that were appearing throughout the long, sleepless nights—thoughts more appealing with each passing day.

In the middle of the night soon after my conversation with Joan, my sense of hopelessness became unbearable. There were no tears, just emptiness. Deciding to move on one idea that had entered my mind, I took the single edged razor blade from its wrapping, sat on the edge of the bed and carefully sliced across one wrist and then the other. It stung just a little, I had not cut deeply and there was little blood. A thought, one I now call an angel thought, let me know I really did not want to die. I wanted help but did not know how to find it. As it turned out, my body finally gave me an ultimatum and Joan did take action on my behalf.

Walking the few blocks to work one Monday morning in September, I sat down at the switchboard, put on my headset and promptly fainted. Joan and another supervisor, Donna, were standing over me as I regained consciousness in the employee lounge. Both wore troubled looks as Joan asked questions.

"How are you feeling? Will you drink some water?"

"Yes, I guess so. Why am I in here?"

Joan explained that I had fainted and that my Aunt Bernice had been called and was coming for me. She had retrieved information from my records, which included a relative's name in the event of an emergency.

"Why?" I asked. "I'm fine"

Donna then spoke up in her best supervisory manner. She would go with me and my aunt to the Y to gather my things and I would stay with Bernice until I felt better. I was too exhausted to argue. Within the hour my aunt arrived and the three of us went to the Y. Somehow I felt a sense of relief. I didn't know what the future held, but it might include help. I could not know then that my work at the telephone company was over.

CHAPTER 35

TURNING POINT

Looking back at this difficult period in my life gives me pause. A part of me asks, *why go over something that happened so long ago and was such a painful experience?* Then I answer my own question: *In the event there is need for deeper forgiveness of anyone or the possibility of gaining new insight, it will be a worthwhile exercise. It may also be of help to someone else suffering from depression. Thus I continue.*

The end of high school and my attempts to move into a new phase called adult living brought to the surface old fears and feelings of inadequacy. Like a vessel holding pain that had reached the top, sorrow had spilled over me. It seemed as if things were moving in slow motion as I gathered my few belongings from the room at the Y and left the building.

The metal door handle felt smooth beneath my hand

as I got in Aunt Bernice's Chevy coupe. On the way to Gourdneck Lake, the landscape seemed as lifeless as I felt. Still, staring out the window, the familiar purr of the car engine brought back pleasant memories. There were many times when the small car had carried my cousins and me on Sunday afternoon drives in the country. I had always liked the car, and now there was something almost comforting about being in it, as if I was protected in a snug cocoon. Although Bernice commented on several neighborhood changes during the drive, I made no response. My thoughts had moved to the question, *what next?*

My aunt's house was kitty corner from Emma and Grandpa's, and as we turned onto the gravel driveway next to the house, tears began building behind my eyes. Relief? Sorrow in the remembrance of happier times in the place? I wasn't sure. My tears hadn't dried up after all. Bernice opened the storm door at the back of the house, which had already been put in place in preparation for the winter months.

"Hold it open, Katie" she said, "I'll get your things." As I did so, she returned to the car and hoisted the suitcase from the trunk, then pulled it along the walkway to the door. Between the two of us we dragged and shoved it up the few steps into the kitchen.

The smell of the house was amazingly familiar, a mixture of brewed coffee, toasted Finnish bread along with Lysol cleaner and other unknown substances unique to the place.

"Do you want something to eat, Katie?"

Nodding in response, she told me to go to my uncle's room first and say hello to him while she fixed coffee and toasted the bread.

My Uncle Harry was the only uncle I would ever know. Momma had told me early on that he was not my real uncle, a familiar message echoed over the years about various family members: *Emma is not your real grandmother, Tony is not your real father, and Harry is not your real uncle.* I had learned to shrug off such comments but did understand that Emma was my uncle's mother and Emma's sister Lempi—Grandpa's first wife—was Momma's mother. So Harry was Momma's step-brother. He spent most of the time in bed due to crippling rheumatoid arthritis. He had begun to show signs of it as a teenager and now could not turn his head or walk without crutches. I had always liked my uncle even though he enjoyed teasing me at times.

"What happened?" he asked me. I didn't answer. What could possibly be said to help him understand what I could not comprehend? Shrugging my shoulders I left his room to go back to the kitchen. The toasted Finnish bread smelled so delicious I actually felt hungry for the first time in many weeks. Sitting at the small kitchen table and looking out the window while eating, I noticed the leaves on the giant oak in the back yard just beginning to change color, another reminder of the winter soon to come. Winter had never been my favorite season. My thoughts were interrupted when Bernice suggested I lie down in the living room. She had phone calls to make and then she would join me there.

I loved my aunt and had always tried to please her. She was never cruel to me, although her method of punishment for wrongdoing, which was shunning, was something to be dreaded. At times I would have no idea what had displeased her. This would cause feelings of confusion and a desire to ask the reason, though I never did. Once, having endured a particularly long period with no eye contact or acknowledgment of my presence, I used some saved coins to buy her a recording of *Peg O' My Heart* by the Harmonicats. It was her favorite song and she showed her appreciation by thanking me many times. Now sitting on her crimson couch with her arms around me, the comfort so longed for led to sleep.

Around four o'clock I heard the squeal of air brakes signaling the arrival of the first bus from Portage Junior High. My cousin Joe would be on it. My uncle had gotten up and was waiting at the door to greet him. What he said chilled me with fear.

"Kate's gone crazy and she's going to a mental hospital."

CHAPTER 36

UNKNOWN TERRITORY

We rode for a while in silence as twilight gradually descended into darkness. Though my thoughts were far from clear, the question did take shape. *Was what my uncle said true? Was I crazy?*

My aunt interrupted my thoughts with a statement that drew me from my reverie.

"Your mother and Tony will meet us at the hospital."

Why in the world would they need to be there? I wondered. Anxiety welled up in me, but rather than ask about them I asked about the hospital. "Where am I going?"

"To a private hospital in Plainwell that was once a tuberculosis sanitarium," she replied. I was glad to hear it wasn't the Kalamazoo State Hospital. Everyone knew about that place. Some said it was like the hospital in the movie "Snake Pit." I had summoned up the courage to go there a few months back in hope of finding help for the dark feelings that engulfed me. I'd been given the Rorschach Test and told to come back in a week, but I didn't follow through.

Bernice returned to the subject of Momma and Tony.

"They have to be there since we're not sure of your insurance coverage, and you may need help in paying the bill." I could have laughed but didn't. Tony didn't keep his commitments and would not pay the bill. I didn't want to think about that now and said no more.

The three-story Victorian house was only partially visible in the moonless night when we arrived. Walking up the steps and through the main entrance, Bernice and I found Momma and Tony sitting in a wide foyer near an open office door. They got up and greeted us, Momma looking anxious and Tony standing with his hands stuck palms down in the back pockets of his pants as he often did, his face devoid of expression. *Had anything changed about him*? I gave them each a half-hearted hug.

As if on cue, a woman came through the open door and directed us into her office. Questions came next.

"Age?"

"Eighteen."

"Present address?"

Nowhere, I thought. Momma offered the South Burdick Street address where they were still living.

"Who will be responsible for the cost of the stay?" Tony spoke up with a tone of assurance. "I will."

The woman asked him to sign his name on the

bottom of a document, which he did. His signature would mean nothing to him.

The woman then asked about my symptoms. I did not like talking about this with Momma and Tony present and waited for her to be more specific.

"What do you mean?" I asked.

"Are you eating and sleeping well?"

"No," I answered.

"Have you ever thought of suicide?"

"Yes."

There were more questions, and then she said, as if to herself, "Sounds like depression."

Depression. I had heard the term before. *Depressed, not crazy,* I thought.

Before we left her house, Bernice had told me I would not need the things in my suitcase and could get them later. When the woman asked for any possessions, saying they would be kept in a safe place and returned to me when I left the hospital, I had only my purse to give her. But a small stirring of hope passed through my mind when she said, *leave the hospital.*

A man in a white uniform stood in the foyer as we left the office. He had come to take me to my room on the third floor. I said my good-byes to Momma, Tony, and Bernice and walked beside him to an elevator at the end of the hall. It looked like ones in a recent movie, similar to a telephone booth but made of wood and large enough for two or three people. Once on, the uniformed man pulled two lattice-like metal doors together, and with a jerk we began to move upward.

Having reached the third floor, yet another person greeted me—a nurse also in white who led me to an enclosure with a counter, the nurses' station. Across from it an open door revealed an attractive bedroom occupied by an older man who was reading a newspaper. He looked up and, seeing me, his eyes and mouth took on a smirking expression. I felt some reassurance about the place after seeing the nice room, but I did not like the man.

The nurse, Miss Collins, took me down a hall with a number of closed doors on both sides, each having an area of crisscrossed wood about eight inches square a little above eye level. This, I would discover, was the only way to see in or out of the room. A light fixture was attached to the wall above each door. "Here we are," she said as she opened a door on the left side of the hall to reveal a space more like a cage than a room. I was stunned, expecting to see a bedroom like the one near the nurses' station. A camp-cot-sized bed attached to the wall and one chair were the only pieces of furniture. To signal a nurse for the bathroom or some other need, I was to push a button located near the bed.

Finally, Miss Collins asked if I had any questions. I shook my head rather than ask the ones that troubled me: *Why does the man I saw as I got off the elevator have such a nice room while this one looks like a cage? Am I a prisoner?* Feeling suspicious for the first time since my arrival, I changed into the plain cotton night shirt Miss

Collins had left for me and, gripped by loneliness, lay on the bed, afraid of what tomorrow would bring.

This must be some sort of trick.

CHAPTER 37

TUESDAY MORNING

For yet another night my brain ran amok with images from the past and fears about what lie ahead. The sound of a key in the lock startled me. A cheery voice belonging to an equally friendly nurse trilled, "So, you're already awake this morning. Good." I said nothing but listened to her instructions to join a group of eight or nine women standing in line at the end of the hall. They all wore night gowns like mine, and soon we would be identically dressed in day dresses, light green in color and non-descript in style.

There was little talking as we waited to go into the bathroom and shower, but several turned my way and smiled as I joined the line. The day nurse, Miss Glover, waited while we showered, donned the green dresses and brushed our teeth. The brushes were to be kept in cubby holes that had our names printed above them. These reminded me of the cloak rooms at Harding Elementary where we tucked our belongings as little kids.

In minutes we were on our way to the dining room with eight tables set for breakfast, four settings with place cards on each table. Finding the one with my given name, Katherine, I joined three women already seated. We exchanged greetings but nothing more. At three of the places sat a small bowl of fruit. The woman whose place was without fruit said nothing about the omission. Her name was Mary. A young man soon brought the next course, eggs, toast and jam. Once again Mary received no food. I wondered why but didn't ask. After all had eaten I did venture a question, "What happens next?" No one answered, but I was soon to discover for myself.

Following the meal Miss Glover walked with me to the office of a psychiatrist, Dr. Jackson. I sat in the chair across from his desk and, being apprehensive, remained perfectly still. He asked several questions, which I did my best to answer, silently wondering what good could come from meeting with him. After a short time he talked into a small box on his desk, asking Miss Glover to return. Dr. Jackson said he would see me tomorrow, and I nodded without speaking.

Arts and crafts, the next activity, were held in a room with several rectangular tables covered with materials that patients were using to make craft items. I selected a project but had little interest in making a basket, or anything else for that matter. One of the women from our table in the dining room sat next to me, and we visited a bit. Her name was Betty and she seemed nice. She asked how I was doing. "Alright, I guess." I answered. Then I blurted out, "Do you have a room that is like a cage?" She said she did and told me to think about my room at home. That's what she did and it seemed to help her.

"I don't have a home," I responded.

"Then imagine one you would like to have one day," she added. I thought that an odd thing to do but would give it a try.

Lunch time and back to the dining room. Sitting down at my assigned place, I noticed again that Mary's place was without dishes or food and now Mary herself was missing. "Where's Mary?" I asked. One woman looked down at her soup bowl. The other two looked at me. Betty, whom I had just talked to in the arts and crafts room, said, "She had a treatment today and now she is resting."

"What kind of treatment?" I asked.

Betty again responded. "They will tell you when you have one. You will know when it is your day because you won't have any breakfast." So I was learning the routine even though I didn't know what a "treatment" consisted of.

Rest time in our rooms followed lunch, and I hoped there would be some activity in the afternoon to again take me out of the cage. As it turned out, we spent much of the afternoon in a large sun room at the back of the house. Comfortable chairs and sofas reminded me of the lobby of the Spa Hotel, except everything here was clean and appeared fairly new. Looking around I could see I was the youngest person present. A woman sat next to me and began a one-sided conversation. Among other things she told me she had no children and that I could be her daughter. This thought did not appeal to me, and, moving to another chair, I decided to avoid her in the future.

Before we were sent back to our cells, a nurse asked us what we liked about the day. I said nothing, really, while a few talked in ways that made little sense to me.

Still, I had made it through the first day.

CHAPTER 38

MY TURN

Did I sleep last night? Even though I was awake before Nurse Glover turned the key in the lock, it seemed to me I had slept for a part of the night. There was a moment of amazement at this thought after so many weeks of sleeplessness.

The routine was a repeat of the day before—bathroom and shower, green patient dress, if it could be called a dress, followed by breakfast. This morning, though, my place at the table was devoid of food, and I asked the women already seated the reason, even though someone had told me the day before.

Betty, who seemed to know the most about the place, answered, "You're getting a treatment today. No food is the sign."

"What kind of treatment?" I asked.

"The doctor will explain," she answered, looking me

in the eyes as if to communicate, ask no more questions.

Watching the others as they ate, including the woman across from me who had missed yesterday's meals, I remembered hearing that she had had a treatment. *She looks alright, but isn't talking much.* I observed. *But what is a treatment?* I would soon find out.

Breakfast was not yet over when a nurse suddenly appeared beside me. Leaning down she said quietly, "Come with me." I had never been hospitalized before and, in fact, had only been to a doctor a few times in my life. Having no idea what to expect, I rose and followed the nurse to a door on the far side of the room. It opened into a long hallway with closed doors on both sides and a row of fluorescent tubes overhead emitting an unnatural light.

When we reached our destination the nurse turned the knob and waited for me to walk past her into the room. Dr. Jackson and another man, who I presumed was also a doctor, stood near a long, brown padded table. Three nurses waited with them. I had never seen so many people dressed in white in one place before. The nurse who had brought me turned and left while the five remaining people watched me walk toward them. Dr. Jackson told me in a kindly way to get on the table and lie on my back. I did so without asking what was to take place, and no explanation was offered. One nurse placed a wide strap with a cold metal buckle across my chest and another strap across my thighs. At the same time small objects were pressed on either side of my temple.

Then a nurse placed a rubber rod about six inches long between my teeth and told me to bite down on it.

What were these people doing to me? I had no idea and was terrified. That was all I remembered.

Shock treatment, no explanation given, just get up on a table when told to do so, bite down on the rubber rod and be shocked out of my senses. As electricity coursed through my body and brain, a grand mal seizure left me unconscious and, I would soon discover, without any memory. I woke up on a cot-sized bed in a place I had not seen before, without knowing what happened, who I was, where I was, or anything of my past that would identify me. Looking around, knowing I was alive but with no idea of who the "I" might be—no memories, no feelings. *Could I speak?* Not sure until I tried and a thin, wordless sound came from my mouth.

How long I remained in this state I don't know. A woman in the room asked how I was feeling. *Who was she? What did she mean?* At some point in the day the faint stirring of memory began to emerge, along with the thought, *I have to get out of here.* As my memory returned I made a decision to do whatever was needed to get out of the hospital. Act cheerful and cooperate despite being in a dark dungeon of uncertainty and fear.

To my great relief my name came back along with other basic information and, to my surprise, I began to feel something taking place inside me. I couldn't say whether it was good or not, it was just different. Sitting in my cell, staying quiet so as not to miss any internal information that might come, I felt better than I had for a long time. Was it due to the decision to be cheerful, as if all was well with me or was there, as it seemed, a tiny pinpoint of light breaking into the darkness?

CHAPTER 39

MY PLACE AT THE TABLE

We are called to many tables in our lifetime: the dinner table, a work table, tables where we join in a game of Monopoly or altar tables where we receive Holy Communion. I was called to the ECT table six times during my stay in the Galesburg Sanitarium. Each treatment, announced by the empty place at the breakfast table, wakened a dreaded anxiety in me. In years to come, patients would be sedated before electricity raced through their bodies and temporarily stole their memories. I would have welcomed such a cushion for my fear.

The summons by the nurse, the walk down the long hall, seeing the thickly-padded table through the open door—the feelings were always the same mixture of fear, resignation and helplessness, held together by my decision: *to do what I had to do to get out of this place.* If this was what it took, so be it. Without being fully aware of it I had taken on a goal, something I had not done in many months. And I had begun the movement out of depression.

At the end of the second week, I began to notice more details in my surroundings, including the people around me. During a Friday therapy session, I scrutinized Dr. Jackson more closely. He was definitely an authority figure but at the same time soft-spoken and kindly in manner. He was shorter than either Grandpa or Tony, had dark hair and brown eyes covered by horn-rimmed glasses, a style popular at that time. After I summoned up the courage to ask him about the treatments, in simple words he said he believed I had been depressed for a long time, so long that my brain had adjusted itself to the condition. The treatments were causing the brain to give up the depressed pattern so health could take its place. The explanation satisfied me at the time. Some years later the main library in Kalamazoo provided me with more information about the treatment. The chemicals in the brain, neurotransmitters that deliver messages from one brain cell to another, begin to work more effectively after a one or two second shock. Since I had not had a physical exam when entering the hospital, I would not learn until later that a thyroid condition may have exacerbated the depression.

By the end of the third week, I began to think about what I would do after leaving the hospital. Nurse Glover was a good listener and, in a way, a confidante as I thought out loud. "Where would I live? With a few hundred dollars in a savings account, enough to get started, I would look for an apartment. What about work? I knew how to find a job. I'd looked for work before and been successful. Would people want to hire me when told about my stay in a mental hospital? Would they have to know?"

Nurse Glover said these were excellent questions. She did not venture to give me answers, however. "Take those questions to Dr. Jackson," she would always say.

The doctor seemed pleased to hear my thoughts about leaving the hospital and gave me some important information. He would like to continue seeing me once a week and would work out a payment plan once I found a job. I had already told him Tony would not be paying the bill, something that did not seem to surprise him.

"I recommend you find a roommate to share an apartment," he added. "While you are looking for your own place you will need to stay with someone in the family." Someone in the family—the thought had not occurred to me. I wouldn't stay with Momma and Tony. Who should I ask, my aunt and uncle or Emma and Grandpa? Dr. Jackson answered my unspoken question for me.

"Do you think your grandparents would welcome you for a short time until you find a roommate and apartment?"

As I hesitated to think about asking them, Dr. Jackson continued. "If you think this would work out, I would like to talk with them and will make the contact." I felt a wave of relief.

Finding a roommate could wait a bit. At the moment, no one came to mind. There was, after all, a stigma attached to people with any kind of mental problem in the 1950s. Had it been a few years in the future, treatment would have been in the form of antidepressant drugs, perhaps without hospitalization. A decade later, after reading the book *I'm Dancing as Fast as I Can* by Barbara Gordon, I would be grateful for the shock treatments rather than drugs. The story of Valium addiction fostered by Ms. Gordon's doctor was a nightmare tale.

As of this writing professionals hold mixed opinions on the use of ECT for depression. Many claim it to be the best treatment for milder cases while others recommend its use only as a last resort. Of one thing I am certain, the treatments helped me.

CHAPTER 40

THE SUBJECT OF GOD

One evening, while I worked on a puzzle in the lounge, the nurse on duty came to me with message: a visitor was waiting to see me. "The night nurse from your floor will be here to get you," she said. I got up from the chair wondering who it could be. Surely it was not Momma or Tony. The rule was no family visits while in the hospital, something I was grateful for.

The night nurse on my floor arrived and together we walked to the elevator to take us to the next floor. Questioning her as to the person's identity gave me nothing more than, "It's a woman. You'll wait in your room while I go to the front desk to bring her upstairs."

After stepping into my cell and hearing the door lock turn, I waited. In a matter of minutes the nurse was back with Jeannette VanderOover.

"Hi, Katie," she said, smiling as she sat down on the

small wooden chair. "How are you doing?"

Years had gone by since I'd seen Jeannette. She hadn't changed much, still wore slightly out of date clothes and a friendly smile. I was in Junior High School the last time I'd visited the flower shop and farm owned by the VanderOovers. Art and Jeanette had always been kind to me and the feelings of affection were mutual. Sitting at their kitchen table eating a freshly-baked cookie with a glass of cold milk had been a childhood treat. They were sweet people. One might think I'd be happy to see her. It was not the case.

After a few awkward moments together she said she had been praying for me. Then reaching into her wool jacket pocket, she pulled out a small maroon book like the one given to me in a Sunday school I had once attended, *The Psalms and New Testament*.

"Could I read some verses to you?" she asked. Though feeling more and more uncomfortable I managed a nod as she opened the book to a place she had marked. She began to read: *Let not your heart be troubled, neither let it be afraid. Believe in God, believe also in me.* (John 14:1)

Suddenly, the discomfort within intensified, becoming a knot in the pit of my stomach. I felt angry, wanting her to leave and she seemed to sense that. Within a minute or two, she put the book back in her pocket and we said our good-byes. A push of the buzzer near the bed summoned the nurse with her key.

What had happened inside me? Why the upset over seeing Jeannette? It didn't take long to recognize embarrassment. I didn't like Jeannette seeing me in this situation in a dinky cell like a prisoner. Then the realization came that God had not come to my thoughts for weeks, even months. Jeanette had reminded me of the questions once asked that were upstaged and set aside by feelings of abandonment: *Why had God let this happen to me? Why hadn't He helped me? I had heard of His love in the Christian Science Church and other churches I had visited. Was I being punished for something God did not like?*

The rush of feelings and the God questions doused any desire to return to the lounge that evening. Lying down instead, eyes fixed on the ceiling and feeling more uncomfortable than I had in some time, another unwelcomed visitor appeared: fear. I hadn't given any thought to where God might be and Jeannette reminded me of that fact. The unanswered questions that mocked me while I stayed at the Y had returned in full force. I decided not to tell anyone about this because anger and fear could mean a longer-than-expected stay in the hospital. In reality my recognition of these feelings was a healthy sign. In the past I tried to avoid what are usually called "negative" feelings. Sometime later I would learn that burying them could be an underlying cause of depression. For now they would not be shared with Dr. Jackson or Nurse Glover or anyone else for that matter.

The window high on the cell's wall soon revealed a wedge of moon in the night sky. The *getting ready for bed* ritual would soon begin. I would not sleep well that night.

CHAPTER 41

LEAVING THE HOSPITAL

I stepped out on the hospital's broad porch that late September morning and felt the crisp autumn air fill my lungs. It was exhilarating despite the fact that anxiety stepped out with me. Having said my good-byes to the hospital nurses who had cared for me the better part of the month along with Dr. Jackson, it was now time to go.

My next appointment with the doctor would be in downtown Kalamazoo at his office on Rose Street. He had called Emma and negotiated an agreement for me to stay with her and Grandpa until I could find work and an apartment. Now ready to get started on the assignments, I opened the door of Aunt Bernice's Chevy coupe once again for the ride to Gourdneck Lake. It was good to see her in her pretty fall jacket over the equally nice dress she had made. She was a good seamstress and had once helped my cousin and me make shorts, which I wore a lot during the summer months. On this trip, decidedly different from the two previous ones, we chatted about the beautiful Indian summer and the activities of the family. She reported all to be well with my two cousins and Uncle Harry.

"Grandpa's been busy caulking around windows and checking the furnaces," she said. "It's hard to believe winter will soon be here."

The car hummed along, a familiar and pleasant sound after several weeks with only limited hospital noises. Soon we turned up the gravel road of Metsa Lane and Grandpa came into view, bent down on his knees in a flower bed, readying the perennials for the cold weather soon to come. I felt a flutter around my heart as tears welled up in my eyes. I had missed him. He raised his head as the car tires crunched up the short gravel incline but there was no wave, just a glance. Dr. Jackson had told me it would be up to me to make changes in my life and not to expect others to be different. So far he was right. Never one for hugs, Grandpa stood now and faced the car as we exited it. There was no luggage to unload since everything of mine had been left in Bernice's care when I entered the hospital.

"Hi, Grandpa," I said. Nodding, he acknowledged me without words. "How are you?" I asked.

"*Mina voin hyvin*," he responded. I nodded, and knew this meant he was fine. Then he pulled a handkerchief out of his coverall pocket and wiped his nose. The space left by his missing finger seemed larger than I remembered. Within moments he returned to his work in the flower beds.

"Your suitcase is in the sunroom," Bernice said through the open car window as she shifted the Chevy into reverse and backed down to her own house a stone's throw away.

"Thank you for picking me up," I called out as she rolled away.

Ah, the sunroom, my favorite place in the house. I often slept there during Finnish get-to-gathers when I was little and recognized a feeling of gratitude to be in this cozy room again sheltered by the large oak tree just outside the windows. When I pulled my navy blue and white-trimmed suitcase off the bed where Bernice had placed it, an indentation remained on the familiar chenille bedspread. Suddenly I felt extremely tired, thought I would lie down for a few minutes, and then promptly fell into a dead sleep. I awoke at two thirty! I couldn't believe I'd slept so long. Ravenous, I headed downstairs in search of food.

The familiar hum of the Frigidaire greeted me before I reached the last step. Opening it, I found pork roast leftovers but decided Emma might have plans for them and chose instead an apple and several slices of rye bread on which I slathered plenty of butter. Taking a place at the familiar red-topped kitchen table I reached for the folded *Kalamazoo Gazette* and briefly scanned an article on the front page about the new leader of the Soviet Union, Nikita Khruschev. History had moved on while I was in the hospital.

The Want Ads in the back were of greatest interest to me. I found several listings under the Jobs column and immediately felt my penchant for organization kick in. Back up the stairs to get paper and pencil to make a list. As was always the case, Emma's desk presented a tidy picture with a pad of paper on one corner of an ink blotter and pencils resting in a chipped coffee mug. I tore out several pages from the tablet then picked out a pencil with telltale marks of a paring knife that had been used to sharpen it. This brought a smile to my face. I wondered if Emma would ever break down and buy a pencil sharpener.

Back to the kitchen table to study the Jobs column and make a list of each possibility with plenty of space for action steps and comments. Soon I had seven on my list, which included a sales clerk position at Gilmores Department Store, an office worker position at Consumer Power Company and an undefined position at a loan company, Instant Money. Next I turned to Apartments for Rent and began a second list. One in Comstock, too far from downtown where I hoped to work; another in Vicksburg, a possibility; Paw Paw, too long a bus ride; and finally one on denBlyken Court just off Burdick Street downtown, a perfect location. This one went to the top of the list.

When I turned to the Personals Column, where I planned to run an ad for a roommate, it occurred to me that someone else might have done the same thing. No luck there, just people looking for other people or ones who left cryptic messages for long lost love interests or friends. After nearly two hours of work I felt the need for a break.

I decided to set the table for dinner first and then take a walk by the lake. Carefully taking the dishes from the cupboard I placed them on the table then selected three each of spoons, knives and forks from the silverware drawer in the kitchen nook. It was then that I ran into my first obstacle and reminder of the shock treatments: *Where to place the different pieces? Did the fork go on the right or left of the plate?* A feeling of panic came over me. *Were there other things I would not remember? What about typing, something I was quite adept at and would likely need in order to get a job? How about math problems,* the telephone numbers once *memorized or the times tables?* I hadn't expected such a simple task to create such anxiety in me.

I put on an old sweater left on a hook by the kitchen door and went out for my walk. *OK, try the times tables.* When I reached 9 x 9 is 81 I breathed a sigh of relief and gratitude that freed me up to enjoy the beautiful autumn day.

I'd had a love affair with nature for a very long time and today, being in it, brought me a deep sense of joy. At the lakeside, with maple and oak trees in full color and a blanket of leaves already on the ground beneath them, I stopped to take in a unique show. As the fast-moving clouds passed over the sun the leaves beneath the trees lay in shadows. In an instant the scene changed, the leaves still clinging to the trees created dancing images on the ground. I stood watching nature's show. Though I had no idea how things would turn out in terms of the job and apartment searches, it felt good to be alive and to be surrounded by such beauty.

CHAPTER 42

FIRST NIGHT OUT

Grandpa had come in from his work while I was outside. He had changed from his work clothes and was walking toward the furnace room just off the kitchen, which was called the "back of the corner." He said little even though I told him of finding some job listings as well as apartments for rent.

Emma came in at about 4:30 p.m. *Would she be glad to see me or a little nervous like I felt about seeing her? She wasn't a hugger so why push it by giving her one?* I thought. Emma cleaned other people's houses and looked tired after a day at Goldman's place, a mansion in my estimation.

"How are you?" she asked

"I'm fine," I replied. "I've found some job openings and apartments for rent in the paper. I'll call in an ad for a roommate tomorrow and then take a bus into town to check on the apartments." It seemed important to let her know I'd be on my way as soon as possible.

"That's good," She replied, and sat down with a reheated cup of coffee left over from breakfast.

I breathed a sigh of relief. I had been more anxious about seeing than I realized. She had seemed so unapproachable to me as a child and I worked hard not to offend her. A memory flashed across my mind to a time when Momma and I had ridden the Greyhound bus to Gourdneck Lake for a visit and Momma had left me with Emma and told me she would be back to get me before dark. She promised, but didn't come back. When it was time to go to bed I vented my little girl anger and told Emma that I knew she was not my real grandmother. There were consequences for my announcement. Emma did not speak to me, except to give directions, nor did she make eye contact with me for the rest of my stay. I felt invisible and came to dread that form of punishment. A spanking would have been easier for a five-year-old to manage. I dealt with two major challenges that day, being lied to and then shunned for expressing anger. But that was then. It was my first day out of the hospital and I had made progress, my lists of job openings and addresses of apartments for rent clear evidence of my success. I felt satisfied.

For dinner that night we had the left-over pork, potatoes, and carrots I'd seen earlier in the day. With little conversation while we ate, my thoughts turned to the remainder of the evening. *What to do? Why, the radio, of course!* The old Magnavox console still stood between the Chesterfield-style chairs in the living room. *But did it work?* Hesitantly, I broached the subject with Emma.

"Do you listen to the radio in the evenings?" Since I knew Grandpa had his own small table-top version in his back-of-the-corner retreat, and that she might listen upstairs, I thought I might join her.

"You can listen to it if you want," she replied. "I had new tubes put in a while back and it works just fine. I have some mending to do on the sewing machine tonight, so you go ahead and use it.

Great, I thought. I would check the radio listings in the *Gazette* after I cleared the table and washed the dishes.

It was Wednesday night and, if I remembered correctly, the *Lux Radio Theater* would be on. *Jack Benny* or *Fibber McGee and Molly* might be airing as well. It was like anticipating an evening with old friends. The radio had been my companion for so many years and I couldn't imagine television ever replacing it in my affection. No need to be worried about that, however. It would be several years before I'd have access to a poor-quality picture and an even poorer story. Of course "I Love Lucy," had not yet been aired. She would become a favorite.

The listing in the paper showed a full schedule of programs. To my delight *Jack Benny* was on with guest star Mickey Rooney. I'd seen all Mickey's and his co-star,

Judy Garland's movies. Never would I have guessed that one day I'd see him in person. Years from now he would star in a musical, "Sugar Babies," in New York City. I would be in the audience, front row far left when he came off the stage and sat on my lap as part of his routine. Talk about thrilled! For now it was enough just to hear his voice and imagine seeing him while I sat in the maroon upholstered chair next to the Magnavox, wrapped in one of Emma's knitted multicolored afghans. It felt soft against my skin. I had not been this comfortable for many months.

By ten o'clock, after mending clothes all evening in her small upstairs study, Emma had begun her nighttime ritual before bed. I felt ready to sleep as well. It had been a fine first day out of the hospital with new possibilities to look forward to in the morning. Soon snuggled in the daybed I looked out at the star-filled sky through the windows next to me, I thought about the past weeks in the hospital. There, I had strained to see the night sky through the small single pane high above my head. Here, I had but to look out a wall of windows to see a nearly-full moon. Tonight I felt light, unencumbered, with thoughts of the day and, more importantly, plans in place for tomorrow.

Then a thought flashed into my head: *Call Sandy Finn.* Her number would be in the phone book. She lived off Burdick Street, a block from the apartment where Momma, Tony, and I had lived in my high school days. Sandy and I had met at the YMCA's Friday night

Canteen and hit it off from the start, becoming good friends. If I remembered correctly, she worked at a business at West Lake on the bus route to Kalamazoo. Maybe we could meet for lunch. She might even know of a job opening. I added this to my mental list of things to do, not forgetting the write-up for the Personal Column for a roommate; I sighed and felt ready for sleep.

I pulled the wool blanket under my chin and before I closed my eyes I felt a sudden urge to say thank you, but to whom, to God? Since being reminded of the Holy by Jeannette VanderOover when she visited me in the hospital, my efforts had been to avoid such thoughts for fear of a return to the uncomfortable place inside. Stories first heard when I went to church with Mrs. Smith, the substitute teacher from elementary school days, stories about God's punishment for sin, must have added to my depression. No, there would be no ruminating about God now. Choosing instead to look out the window at the starlight that glanced around the boughs of the great oak, I offered a thank you to no one in particular and drifted into a peaceful, dreamless sleep.

CHAPTER 43

THE JOB SEARCH

It has been said that the third try is a charm. In Biblical writings the number three is a sign of transition or a significant event about to take place. For example, Jonah was in the belly of the whale for three days, Mary stayed with her cousin Elizabeth for three months, and Jesus was in the tomb for three days. It required two short-lived jobs before finding a right fit on the third try.

A phone call to Sandra Finn led to a job where she worked at the Tri-Lakes Tool and Dye Company. Located on the bus line between Gourdneck Lake and Kalamazoo, it would be easy to reach. Sandy and I arranged to meet for lunch on Saturday at Chicken

Charlie's, our old high school hangout, where she filled me in on Tri-Lakes need for a receptionist. The former one had quit without giving notice, and Mr. Wolfe, the owner, was covering the front desk, taking phone calls and welcoming clients. Sandy worked in the factory area as a supervisor. I was thrilled over the prospect of work so soon after the hospital stay and excited when Sandy said she would try to set me up with an interview for next week.

On the Wednesday after the Monday interview, now as a new employee, I sat behind a large desk that faced double wooden doors with a foyer beyond facing Portage Road. A small table with old copies of *Life* and *Colliers* magazines neatly stacked on it and four unpadded office chairs lined the wall inside the doors. Sandy had trained me on the basics of the job. My employment at Tri-Lakes Tool and Die would last less than a week.

Mr. Wolfe, who looked to be in his fifties, around six feet tall, heavy-set and balding, approached my desk on Wednesday near closing time, laid his hands on my shoulders from behind my chair, and praised me for being a quick learner. He then proceeded to inform me of expectations that were not listed in my job description. To be an employee at Tri-Lakes Tool and Dye would include certain favors, he explained. For these favors I would be paid a bonus. I understood his meaning immediately but was too stunned to speak. I was trapped by his position behind me so that I could not get up and move around the desk to the outside door. In a matter of seconds he released his hands, backed up and said we would talk about the details later. Alone again, I imagined a panicked deer running from a hunter. As I worked to quiet myself I realized what was needed: get on the 5:15 p.m. bus to Gourdneck Lake and don't come back.

I said nothing about what had happened to Emma and Grandpa at dinnertime. The practice of not telling anyone when bad things happened to me had been well developed since childhood. I helped clean up and then walked to Stone's Grocery to use the pay phone outside to call Sandy. It would be too easy for Emma or Grandpa to hear if the call was made in the house. I didn't want that.

The night was clear with the moon rising as I slipped my dime into the phone slot and dialed the number. "Sandy," I said in a near whisper when she answered. "I have to tell you what happened today." After she heard the details, she exhaled loudly.

"Well, now I understand why Sheila, the woman who worked there before you, left. God, he never proposed such a thing to me. What are you going to do?"

"What choice do I have?" I said. "I won't come back. I'll look for another job. I hope there won't be any repercussions for you."

She assured me she would be fine and that there were, after all, other places to work. She needed time to think about what had happened and might look for another job herself. She was sorry I had to go through the experience.

No one else would learn about what had happened. Even though I had done nothing wrong, I felt embarrassed over my short-time employer's actions. *Had I somehow given Mr. Wolfe a message that I would do what he wanted? Maybe he could see I was still a bit uncertain and decided to take advantage of that fact.* I did not sleep well that night.

It wasn't until 1991 when Clarence Thomas was being considered for Supreme Court Justice and Anita Hill accused him of sexual harassment, that I let myself feel the pain over the encounter at my first job after hospitalization. I wept bitter tears over my limited choices back then, the limited choices of all women at that time in history. Sexual harassment laws had not as yet been considered.

My second position was with Instant Money at the corner of Walnut Street and Portage Road. The ad in the Help Wanted column was short and to the point: *Small company needs person to receive loan payments. Good hours.* It was a five-person operation in a storefront next to the Harley-Davidson motorcycle shop. The office included a bench for waiting customers, a counter behind which I would sit or stand, and a door that was kept locked between the customer area and the back where four people worked at desks. I would help customers fill out loan requests and collect money from those who came in to pay back what they owed.

It didn't take long to see what kind of a business it

was. The borrowers who came in to pay off their debt were poor. Most, but not all, were Negroes (the term 'African Americans' had not yet come into use to describe people of color). The interest rate on the loans was so high that very little of a payment went toward the principle. I would take their small loan books, enter the amount paid and initial the entry. The amount owed did not change much. It would take many months to pay off even a small loan. The borrowers must have needed cash badly to have agreed to the terms. Appalled, I knew that I could not be a part of such an operation. *Weren't there laws to protect people from this sort of thing,* I wondered? I quit. Sad to say such operations are still in our communities' today taking advantage of people most in need of financial help.

On the next Monday morning Consumer's Power became the third company I approached for a job. I'd seen their ad for workers needed in Billing and Accounts Receivable and took the bus to town to apply. After I entered their building on Rose Street, next door to the YWCA, my temporary home before I entered the hospital, I could see several other young women in the waiting room outside the office where we would apply. We sized each other up and likely wondered together who might land the jobs. The interview went well. I had not told them I'd been in a mental hospital due to depression.

CHAPTER 44

A PLACE TO CALL HOME

Next on the agenda: a place to live. When the interview at Consumer's Power was over there was plenty of time to look at apartments before the bus left for Gourdneck Lake. I actually had only one on my list which was just blocks away. Despite the fact that no one had answered my ad in the Personals Column for a roommate, it seemed the right time to leave Emma's and Grandpa's. Perhaps it was my imagination but, Emma didn't seem to like the arrangement agreed upon with Dr. Jackson. I would run the want ad for a roommate again over the weekend.

I had called the number listed in the ad and got directions for an upstairs apartment on denBlyken Place. It was an easy walk from Consumer's Power to the tree-lined cul-de-sac just off Burdick Street. The five two-story houses on the street with their neat lawns and large shade trees looked quite pleasant, far nicer than many places I'd lived with Momma and Tony. Within seconds I found number 302, the house with the apartment for rent. Climbing the steps to the front porch I felt a wave of excitement sweep over me. This might be the place. It was confirmed when Mrs. Nelson, the landlady, answered the door and led me upstairs to a three-room, nicely furnished space, just right for working girls.

The kitchen looked down on the street in front with a cozy living room next to it. The bedroom held two identical twin beds, a dresser, and an old fashioned stand-up mirror. I fell in love with the place and, even though I had not yet been hired by Consumer's Power, I gave Mrs. Nelson a cash deposit along with the assurance there would be a roommate. I said good-bye to her and walked to the Greyhound Bus Station to catch the bus back to the lake feeling confident I would get the job as well as find a room-mate.

To my delight the ad I'd placed in the Sunday paper for a roommate was answered soon after my return to Emma and Grandpas that Monday afternoon. A young woman from Newaygo near Grand Rapids, Sharon Adams, told me about herself, her work at a company in the downtown area, her fiancé, who was in the Army and stationed in Korea, and the fact that she was staying with a friend of her grandmother's on the other side of town. We arranged to meet at Schuler's Cafeteria on Tuesday after she got off work then go see the apartment together. It was a match and the onset of a friendship. We moved in together the following weekend but not before I heard from Consumer's Power. I got the job!

It was possible to move from Emma and Grandpa's on the bus since I had so little to carry. I boarded the early-morning Greyhound on Saturday after saying good-bye and thanking them for letting me stay with them. I had stopped by my aunt and uncle's the night before to thank them for their help as well. No sad leave-taking since no one was unhappy. In fact it was just the opposite. For my part, there was a wonderful feeling at being on my way. Emma and Grandpa probably felt relieved. I guessed they were afraid of my needing ongoing help as Momma had needed over the years. Now the bus ride gave me a chance to think about the things that needed to be done in my very own apartment.

Sharon was already upstairs when I arrived at our new place and we went right to work deciding on the division of drawers and closet space and then stowing our things. By late morning, Sharon left for the grocery store and I had donned my rather outdated blue coat for a trip to buy kitchen and bathroom items at F. W. Woolworth. It was a short walk just four blocks down Burdick. I walked briskly in the cool autumn air wondering if the young man who was a student at Western Michigan still worked there. My memory was that he'd gone back to his hometown during the summer months because of illness. I doubted I would see him. As it turned out, Doug DeGrow walked toward me within minutes of entering my old work place. We stood near the front of the store between aisles exchanging pleasantries.

"How have you been? I heard you had been ill. Was that this past summer or the year before?" As soon as I asked I wondered if I was too bold in doing so.

"The summer before," he responded. "What about you? How have you been?"

"Well, I had a bit of difficulty this fall, was in the hospital most of September."

Thankfully he didn't ask why and I didn't offer any details. That would come later.

Near the close of our brief visit he asked me out, quite a surprise since I had stood him up many months before. Along with a nervous laugh, I said yes and promised to be at our apartment when he arrived on Friday night. A phone had not yet been installed so I quickly wrote down the denBlyken address and we said our good-byes. That first date, followed by many more in the two years that followed, led to engagement and marriage. I never could have imagined it.

My life with Doug would require a whole other book. Suffice to say he has been my love for nearly six decades, traveling with me through the many stages of marriage and being the kind of father to our children I would have loved to have. We have learned from each other—the art of compromise, the giving and receiving of care, sharing joys as well as helping each other through times of grief.

He is a precious man.

CHAPTER 45

DIFFICULT GOOD-BYES

Doug received his draft notice the day before our wedding in July of 1955. Thankfully he waited to break the news until after the big day when we were on our honeymoon at Lake Michigan. Devastated, a thought began to dominate: *I should have known this was too good to be true.* He was to report to Ft. Leonard Wood in Missouri in three short weeks. "What next?" I wondered aloud. It was a good and necessary question.

Together we decided to talk to his sister, Marge, who had come from Florida for Doug's graduation from Western Michigan and our wedding a month later. If she was open to it I would travel to Florida with her, find a job, and later be reunited with Doug at the Army base to which he was assigned. That would work. When we returned to our apartment in Kalamazoo and talked to Marge the three of us worked out a plan for me to join her on her trip south. She liked the idea since she wasn't thrilled about driving the long distance alone. It was easy to see she felt sorry about Doug being drafted so soon after we were married and was happy to help in this way. She hoped I'd want to go to Tarpon Springs where she lived and taught school. I could room with her and find a job in the area. It sounded like a good plan to all three of us.

It was early August, the day before his twenty-third birthday. Doug had boarded the bus with other draftees bound for Ft. Leonard Wood for the first leg of basic training while I stood on the sidewalk and watched the men move down the bus aisle and select their seats. There were no tinted windows then to obstruct the view so I could see him move into a place next to a window near where I stood. I felt devastated but tried to perk up and smile at him. Marge, who had said her good-byes and waited a short distance from the bus, came to stand with me after I motioned for her. We waved as the bus pulled out of the station and down Portage Road on its way to Missouri.

Contact with Momma and Tony had been sporadic since I left the hospital. They had come to the wedding and we were together at Gourdneck Lake several times. Momma seemed to have adjusted to my absence over the past several years and the next morning I would say good-bye again for what would likely be a long time. She knew about Doug's notice from Uncle Sam and had handled the news fairly well when I last talked to her—something that now gave me a level of comfort. I did hate to see her upset. Once again Marge had driven me and in a short time we were parked in front of the two-story, frame house.

We entered the hall Momma had told me to take and then looked for number nine. My knock brought a quick response as the door opened. She greeted us and then motioned us to come in, all without making eye contact. Her nice cotton dress included an added touch, a rhinestone pin worn near the collar. She wasted no time with an invitation to sit on a davenport that had seen better days. I recognized the offer of a cup of coffee as her sign of welcome and received it gladly. Marge did as well. Momma went into the kitchen and brought us, one at a time, coffee in mugs that did not match. I was touched. *Not the time for tears,* I thought.

We talked a little about what I would do in Florida and I promised to write to her. She said she would try to do so too. That I doubted. Tony had come into the room from what I thought must be the bedroom. He listened but didn't enter into the conversation at first. After about 15 minutes we got up to leave and Momma gave me a hug, which I returned. My tears commenced and Momma looked uneasy. She never was comfortable with my tears or her own for that matter. Tony kept his hands facing forward in his back pockets as was his habit and wished us good luck. *The visit had gone well*, I thought. The hard part would come several days later when Marge and I drove to Gourdneck Lake to say good-bye to Emma, Grandpa, my aunt, uncle, and cousins.

Early the next morning Marge arrived at the apartment Doug and I called home for just three short weeks. Her new red and white 1955 Pontiac had plenty of room for our belongings and, after a quick breakfast at a diner near downtown, we were on our way to the lake. Within the hour I stood on Metsa Drive once again with the August air warm on my skin. Family came out of their houses to stand with us on the lush grass Grandpa so carefully tended. It was a beautiful day. A bit of small talk commenced. *Nice car, you got there, Marge. How does she drive? How long will you be on the road?* There were no questions about gas mileage then since it cost 25 cents a gallon and was plentiful.

The hoped-for blessing and wish for a safe journey were not forthcoming. What I did hear left me with feelings of guilt that would stick like glue and travel with me for many years. Grandpa's parting words came in the form of another kind of question, "Katie, who is going to take care of your mother now?" It was an awkward moment as conversation stopped and the words hung in the air like a sopping wet towel on a clothes line. Marge as yet knew little of my past or my relationship with

Momma and Tony. That would change over the years as I shared my story but for now she was left to wonder about Grandpa's question. As for me...I could not give him an answer.

CHAPTER 46

CHANGES AND MORE CHANGES

The decade that began with our marriage turned out to be a whopper. I took Marge's invitation to share the room she had rented in Tarpon Springs, a charming Greek community on Florida's west coast noted for its sponge docks and Sponge Exchange. My job search commenced soon after we arrived since the check I would receive as a soldier's wife, a dependent, would be a while coming. I had begun to feel anxious over the amount of money I had left. By that time I was also pretty sure I was pregnant. A wave of panic at life moving so quickly swept over me on some days, but having the goal of finding a job helped me to stay focused. I would have been happy to work at one of the small shops that catered to tourists at the sponge docks but found none to be available. In fact the only job opening in town was a so-called secretary at the Tarpon

Zoo, a small operation just outside the city limits on Highway 19. It turned out to be a kind of clearing house for tropical birds and snakes from Central and South America. Several features proved to be both interesting and challenging. I couldn't say they were pleasant, however.

The owner of the zoo, a woman named Trudy, had a pet chimpanzee she named Susie. She treated the cute, furry creature as if she was a human toddler that wore diapers, was fed from her special dish with a spoon, and allowed to play in the office with specially-chosen educational toys. If I took the job I would be expected to look after this little anthropoid when Trudy was busy or away from the zoo. I was promised it would never be for an extended period of time. I agreed to begin the job the very next day.

It turned out there was a problem from the onset. Susie the chimp did not like me and I didn't care much for her either. She would scream that awful chimp scream, grab at my clothes, and even try to bite me at times. I loved animals but her behavior was just not acceptable and I wasn't at all sure this job would work out. I'd have to see.

The second challenge was my desk located in a large room where visitors to the zoo were welcomed, and on two sides glass enclosures held snakes—yes snakes. I would look to one side and the back to see what they were doing. Actually I wanted to be sure they were all in their right place. The young men who worked at the zoo walked through the office a number of times my first day rather than go around the building on the outside. I later realized they were checking things out and, in the process, got an inkling of my nervousness about the snakes surrounding me. Then on the third day they thought they'd have a little fun at my expense.

Back then the latest model of the Remington typewriter could be found in most offices and this one was no exception. Trudy had told me to cover it at the end of the day with the fitted jacket that came with the machine. On the third morning I came through the side door and found several of the young men there chatting with one another. I greeted them and then went to the desk, put my purse in a drawer, and lifted the cover from the machine. I screamed. A snake was wrapped around the typewriter. The workers thought it to be a good joke and laughed with great gusto. I, in turn, let them know it was not funny and that I would speak to Trudy about it when she came in. One of the jokesters then took the creature to return it to its domain. As for me, I was shaken.

The next morning I hesitantly entered the office, looked right and left, then took hold of the typewriter cover and lifted it while jumping back at the same time. To my relief no snake was there to greet me. I began my work, though a bit jittery, as one might expect. About midmorning I looked straight in front of my desk to one of the two doors into the building. To my horror a boa constrictor slid silently through the space and into the room. *Oh my God,* I thought as I leaped up and headed for the side door to my left. At that moment one of the young men came in carrying a pole with a hook attached to one end along with a large gunny sack. He very adeptly gathered up the creature and deposited it in the sack. Now outside the door I let him know I was angry, thinking it to be another lame joke. He responded to my rebuke with an explanation. The cover of the snakes pit had been left off the night before, the snake had decided to explore the area and when Trudy had heard what happened she told him to find it and get it back in its place. That was it, and it was also the last day of yet another job. I left the zoo and walked the short way to the bus stop for the ride back to Tarpon Springs. One good thing I took from that experience was my awareness of snakes being held captive in small glass enclosures. How unnatural for them. I also wondered why so many people like me feared snakes. I guessed it went back to the Adam and Eve story.

Doug's mother, Vera DeGrow, had told me I was welcome to stay with them in Jacksonville if things didn't work out in Tarpon Springs. With no other job prospects in the Tarpon Springs area I decided to accept the kind offer. Marge and I had already made plans to go to her parent's home over Labor Day so I ran my idea past her and then phoned Vera. She seemed happy that I would be staying with them until Doug received his assignment.

The gratitude I felt over being with Vera and Russell was for good reason. They owned a motel just south of the Georgia state line on Highway 1 and I could work with the housekeeping crew made up of Vera, a cousin named Margaret, and a woman named Vesta, who worked part-time. That would help pay for my keep until my government checks came. I would find a doctor there to confirm what I already knew. Vera and Russell would be grandparents again.

The next few months would be the first time I felt part of a family who expressed love and affection for each other. Vera was a no-nonsense kind of woman honest and straight forward about the work I could do to help with the motel operations and quick to express gratitude for what I did. From the onset of our time together she agreed to my request to call her "Mom." My father-in-law, Russell was a quiet man, kind and quick to notice when something needed to be fixed or tended. My time with them became a peaceful interval amid change.

CHAPTER 47

TOGETHER AGAIN

Doug was assigned to a base in El Paso, Texas and that meant we could be together again. We were grateful since parenthood was fast approaching. After Lynda's birth at the Fort Bliss Army Hospital, he was sent to Italy for a year while she and I moved back to Florida to live with his parents. Though I was sad to be separated from Doug again—this time for a year—there was a bright spot. It was a great experience living with a stable family, a family that seemed more and more like one I'd always wished for. Vera was delighted to have a precious granddaughter and agreed to care for Lynda when I found a job. I soon was employed at Prudential Insurance located on the river near downtown Jacksonville. A star on the calendar marked the day Doug was expected back in the states.

One year later he not only returned home but was

discharged from the Army. His first job with General Electric Investments began in Jacksonville, followed by a transfer to West Palm Beach and later to Miami. During a six-year period two more little ones arrived, son Russell and daughter Amy.

Throughout those years episodes of depression showed up that frightened me. This was especially the case after the birth of each child. There was no mention of post-partum depression at that time. I don't think it had yet been identified. When I learned about the disorder I was sure it described my situation. Doug would often feel stymied as to how to handle it and, had it not been for the children, I might have despaired with each dreaded recurrence. They were beautiful, bright children who had to be cared for and, since I lacked much experience or knowledge in child-rearing, I did what I had done all my life. I found help from a librarian at the Public Library, Benjamin Spock's, *The Common Sense Book of Baby and Child Care*. I renewed it as long as allowed and then bought my own copy, using it until pages became dog-eared and began falling out.

A second resource was discovered on the library shelf as well, Norman Vincent Peale's *The Power of Positive Thinking*. His message was akin to what I'd heard at the Christian Science Church when going with Miss Miller as a young girl: mainly, that our thoughts are not neutral but are either positive and life-giving or negative and harmful. I worked mightily to hold to peaceful, positive ones despite the inner demand of depression to do otherwise.

Two goals dominated my thinking; to do a better job of parenting than Momma and Tony had given me and to avoid being hospitalized again.

During this time in the Miami area we became members of a United Methodist Church not far from our home. The three children seemed happy in their Sunday school classes and I decided to join a women's Bible study group that met during the week in member's homes. I read the Bible occasionally, after hearing a new idea presented in a Sunday sermon, but didn't study it on a regular basis. *The study group could be interesting. After all, the Bible was a collection of books and I loved books.*

The women in the group were all older than me, had children—some even grandchildren. Together we read and discussed individual books and themes found in scripture and talked about how they applied to our lives. I had loved the Bible stories I'd heard as a child and began to recognize messages that could help me in my daily life.

The history of Israel also began to impress me. I recalled when, on my thirteenth birthday in 1948, Israel became a state. I'd seen newsreel films of people entering Palestine and recalled a teacher at Washington Junior High talking about it in class, telling us the land the Jews had once called home would become one again for many who had survived the death camps during the war. I felt tearful at recalling this, reminded of the story I'd first heard at Harding Elementary about the long journey the people had made to reach the Promised Land with Moses as their leader. It seemed right for them to return to Palestine.

The time spent with the group talking and studying together, along with the reading I had begun to do on my own, fascinated me. I learned that the Old Testaments, Jewish scripture, held books by prophets who showed courage and determination to follow the Law given them by God. I came to love many of the Psalms as well, ones that called out to God in times of trouble and others expressing praise and thanksgiving.

A resource used in the group, William Barclay's *The Daily Study Bible Series*, became a teacher for us. Together we discovered history, parables, allegories, genealogies, etiologies (stories that answered questions) and letters. Who would have thought there were so many kinds of writings in the Bible! My image of Jesus began to change as a result of what I was reading as well. I had thought of him as a loving man, a healer and friend of children but at the same time rather timid and, what one woman in the group called, milquetoast. He was not that at all! I was just beginning to comprehend the meaning of his life and message. I'm still at it.

A deeper love for scripture began in that group and continues to this day. My gratitude for the women I came to know, Martha, Virginia, Helen, and the others

who were there to support me in July of 1963 when
Momma died.

CHAPTER 48

WHERE'S MOMMA?

The cause of her death: a stroke. The call came on a Sunday afternoon while I stood outside in the hot Miami summer and pushed the Jungle Gym swing for our son, Rusty. Phones were attached to walls in those days and Doug had put down the Sunday *Miami Herald* to answer ours. He called for me to come with a bit of an edge in his voice, something not often heard. I came through the back door to take the call, the voice on the other end seemed somewhat familiar and yet I couldn't quite place it for a moment. It was Tony. I had never talked with him on the phone before. He was crying when he told me Momma had died but quickly pulled himself together to give me the details.

"The doctor said there was no chance of her living. The stroke ruined her. Emma and Grandpa were there when he told us. We all knew it."

"You were in her room where she could hear?" It was as though I wanted to avoid the reason for his call and instead concentrate on specific details.

"Yes, we were all in her room but she wasn't conscious. She couldn't hear," he responded.

I had recently read that people in that condition might indeed be able to hear; I felt a shudder go through me. The shock over of her death coupled with the thought of them discussing her condition in her presence was more than I could handle. My legs started to buckle and Doug, who stood at my side, took hold of me and simultaneously grabbed the phone with his other hand putting it to his ear. Tony told him they would wait for me to come to handle the funeral arrangements, something he thought I needed to do.

I thought I needed to do it too, and left the next day on an Eastern Airlines DC 10 out of Miami International Airport. It was an afternoon like so many others in the summer months. As I walked out on the tarmac to board the plane I could see fast moving dark clouds to the north. Once inside and seated with the other passengers, a turbulent lightning storm commenced. Just a few miles out, while still gaining the desired altitude, flashes of light broke through the clouds as the plane rocked and heaved. They matched my own internal state. *I should have listened to Doug when he insisted on going in my place*, I thought. I had argued instead that I must do this one last thing for Momma. Now my refusal of help resulted in white knuckles as I clutched the arm rests and we bumped our way through the clouds. I prayed mightily that we would not be struck by lightning. What was I thinking when I decided to make this trip! Later I would learn that persons who are not adequately cared for in childhood often do not give themselves good care as adults.

Once we had reached an altitude above the storm, my inner turmoil quieted and my thoughts turned to questions that had begun to trouble me, deep questions of faith, as some called them. Momma's death injected a kind of urgency to my desire for answers. *If there was life beyond this earthly one, as was declared in the Affirmation of Faith each Sunday at church, where was Momma now? Was there a heaven and a hell?* Since my thoughts provided no satisfactory answers I turned to more practical matters…the funeral, what it would be like and how I would get through it. In fact, I had not as yet been to a funeral service. It would be my first.

The service, held two days later, did not provide any answers to my questions about heaven and hell but rather left me with more frustration and sadness. The officiating preacher was one the funeral director called on for the deceased who were not active in a church or have a pastor of their own.

The day of the service came and, as I sat on a thinly

padded funeral home chair, I looked at the minister who stood before a small group of family members and a few friends. I listened for words that would answer my question about where Momma might be. These few who had gathered on that hot summer's day, like me, may have wondered what he would say about Momma. In fact, there was little reference to her but rather a message about our need to be saved, which would assure us a place in heaven.

This theology I heard was not new to me. It sounded like sermons preached at some churches I had attended as a young girl. Nothing was said about Momma and her struggles in life or of a merciful God who loved her. There really wasn't much the preacher could say about her life since he had never met her or visited with any of the family in order to learn more. If he had known Momma would he have talked about her need to be saved since she never went to church and wasn't one to follow acceptable rules? Even though I supposed the service might have been worse, the anger in me increased as I listened to his words.

After the service everyone was invited to Gourdneck Lake. Emma and Grandpa no longer lived in the house next to the lake but rather in a smaller one they owned and used as a rental on Portage Road. We sat on metal lawn chairs drinking lemonade and making small talk about the weather or politics. I said nothing about my feelings since I didn't think I could hold back my tears and anger about the service. It was a difficult afternoon. I felt relieved when it was over.

CHAPTER 49

QUESTIONS ANSWERED WITH QUESTIONS

The next morning Emma left the house to get groceries while I tidied up after breakfast. It seemed strange to be in this new space with pieces of furniture I remembered from childhood. The red-topped kitchen table with its red padded chairs still held a place of prominence even in a much smaller and less airy kitchen. The aroma of brewed coffee and cardamom bread hung in the air. That part had not changed either. I appreciated these sensate reminders in the unfamiliar house.

I looked out the kitchen window while I rinsed the dishes and noticed a cardinal perched at the neighbor's birdfeeder, its mate in a nearby bush waiting a turn. These beauties were not seen in our Miami neighborhood and the sight of them gave me a sense of comfort. Birds were one of God's dearest creatures as far as I was concerned. *Remember to tell the children when I talk with them today. They've never seen cardinals. I wonder what they are doing this morning?* A mental picture of the kids at play in the back yard or in their rooms brought up a longing to see them. I'd be going home the next morning and was happy that was the case.

It was then that another sort of question came to me as if from nowhere. *"Did you love your mother?"*

For a moment I stood still, the cup in my hand poised in mid-air. The inquiry seemed like my own thought yet something felt different as though the words were encircled in a cocoon of silence. The question was clear and focused with nothing to invade the protective margins, unlike so many that troubled me, ones that tumbled into my mind one after another. I felt something unusual was taking place.

Yes, I did. I loved her.

Silence, then a second question still circled in silence.

"You loved her after all the pain and neglect you experienced as her child?"

Again, I had to think for a moment. I wanted to be honest with myself, I answered.

Yes, I loved her. I still love her.

Then the thought that relieved me of the fearful questions about Momma, *"You love her despite the pain. The infinite God loves her even more."*

A wave of peace came over me as I clung to the words, not wanting to lose a bit of their sweetness, tears filled my eyes. *Forget the preacher's message at the funeral. God loves Momma.*

Soon after Emma returned from the grocery store and the day progressed without my mention of the cardinals or my morning inspiration. However, one more revelation would take place before the day was over.

CHAPTER 50

AN IMPORTANT ANSWER

Movie ratings didn't begin until the 1960s. The majority of films were free of overt violence and sex at that time so when I entered the State Theatre as a young teen I didn't know I was in for a shock. The film was not a western or one of those extravaganzas that featured Fred Astaire and Ginger Rogers. It was "Johnny Belinda" starring Jane Wyman. She'd won an Oscar in 1948 for her role in the poignant story of a young woman who was deaf and mute. Belinda was raped and subsequently gave birth to a son whom she named Johnny: I was traumatized by the film. In the years that followed I had nightmares of the rape scene and would wake in sweats. The story touched a deep place within as if it had to do with me. There was no way I could know that Momma's funeral and the story I was about to hear would explain my reaction and help me better understand Momma.

The groceries had been carried in and put away and now Emma and I sat at the kitchen table with yet another cup of coffee and my favorite Finnish bread while Grandpa was out working on a fix-up project. Emma repeated a comment she had made after the funeral when she said she hadn't cared for the minister's message. I nodded but did not add anything about my own feelings. If I were to do so the anger I felt over the message might be reignited. I didn't want to lose my current sense of comfort. As Emma got up to pour a second cup of coffee for each of us she said,

"I have something to tell you, something that took place a long time ago. It's about your Mother."

What about her? I wondered.

"I should have told you years ago, but just couldn't seem to do it."

I realized for the second time that day that something important was taking place. I became very quiet, ready to hear what she had to say.

"It was in August when your Mother went to a dance at Long Lake."

These words held no surprise. I knew Momma loved to dance. When I was a little girl I loved to see her at the Finnish parties. I knew where the band shell and pavilion were at Long Lake as well. It was a good place to play hopscotch and jump rope, things I often enjoyed as a child. Bands still played there on Saturday nights during my high school days.

Emma continued. She wasn't sure who Momma went

to the dance with, it may have been Tony.

"He had come from the Netherlands, but we didn't know much about him then." She continued.

No, it would not have been unusual for Momma to be at Long Lake dancing on a summer night. I continued to listen intently until the jarring words were spoken.

"Your mother was raped, not by one man alone but several."

She went on to tell me that Momma had been beaten as well. She had come home in the early morning hours with her clothes ripped and places already turning black and blue on her arms and face. It would be a while before she or any of the family knew she was pregnant with me.

With this announcement I felt as cold as the coffee that remained in my cup. I wished for something to break the stillness but instead sat silently. It would take a few minutes for me to process the revelation, and yet somehow it was as if I'd always known. My attempts to protect her as a child suddenly made sense to me. Being raped made her like Belinda in the movie I'd seen so long ago. She had been defenseless, with no voice of her own and vulnerable, just as Momma always seemed to be.

The following spring, just weeks before my birth, Tony and Momma married. I followed Momma's direction and never called him daddy because she told me he wasn't my real father. The fact was, she didn't know who fathered me. No wonder she couldn't answer when I asked, *Where is my daddy?*

Emma went on to tell me that Momma had been

sterilized after my birth. To Emma's knowledge she had not been consulted on the procedure. The doctors had, however, talked with Grandpa and the decision made, she would never have another child.

After hearing the story the two of us stayed seated at the table in silence. As we did, the sound of the cardinal I'd seen in the morning came through the open window. It came as a comfort just as it had earlier.

Emma seemed relieved to have told me the story and repeated what she said about Momma not knowing about the surgery beforehand. *How could that be?* I wondered. It seemed to me a woman should be consulted about such a thing.

The remainder of the day gave me time to think, to grieve over Momma's death and the story I'd heard. I decided to cross Portage Road and go to a familiar place beside the lake. There, the waves gently lapped at the pier and I remembered the hours I spent there as a child. I was sorry about what happened to Momma; sorry she had had such unhappiness in her life. Then remembering the experience earlier in the day, I thanked God for loving her. It would be awhile before I looked into sterilization laws in this country. I was shocked at my findings.

CHAPTER 51

UNCOVERING THE FACTS

Making my way to the Public Library to do research on the subject of eugenics, the term used to define the sterilization of "undesirables," led to surprising information. My youthful naiveté was still present when I began reading that forced sterilization was legal in many parts of the world, including 35 of our United States. *Would our country really do that?* I asked myself. But there was even more to the story.

Apparently the United States was quite successful in carrying out the law since history tells us Adolf Hitler himself praised us for our handling of *the problem,* people who were inadequate or impaired. He had implemented the term *survival of the fittest,* a phrase attributed to English philosopher Herbert Spencer and adopted by Charles Darwin, to define his concept of natural selection. Darwin's use of the term, however, had nothing to do with the handicapped, the so-called feeble-minded, the depressed, prostitutes, which included women who had sex out of wedlock, and, ultimately, the elimination of the world's Jews. It had nothing to do with social engineering or the breeding practices of the poor but proved a useful vehicle in the hands of Hitler and social engineers in our own country as a means for handling *the problem.*

The practice of forced sterilization was employed on thousands of people who, through misfortune or behavior unacceptable to society, became victims of state governments. I remembered seeing state-owned buildings at a facility named Wahjamega located near the main highway through Caro, Michigan. Children and young people who were, or thought to be, epileptic were housed there. Parents feared that a child with a history of seizures, or ones who had experienced a seizure brought on by a fast-rising temperature, might lead to his or her removal from the home and placement in the facility with sterilization to follow. At the same time many children with severe convulsive episodes were said to have been on waiting lists for a place in the institution. It was safe to assume that Momma had been considered an undesirable because of depression, learning disabilities, and being the victim of rape thus requiring her sterilization. She should have had the right to decide her own fate and the help needed in making the decision.

Until that time I had not given much thought to the

issue of abortion or to the angry words used by Momma during times of stress, "I didn't want you." *Had she wanted to abort me?* It would be many years until my trip to Finland and learning of Lempi's death as a result of the then illegal procedure in 1913. There was no thought on my part to question Emma and Grandpa about it now. I did ask myself, *would Grandpa have condoned Momma having an abortion after what happened to his young wife so many years ago?* I guessed not. With the newfound information to process and now feeling a real sense of gratitude for my having been born, I felt grateful to be here.

It is a fact that the abortion issue which has resulted in so much dissention in our country is not a simple one. It requires our best thought and highest level of compassion for both the woman and the developing fetus. My would-be grandmother lost her life due to an abortion and my mother who was ill-equipped to raise a child and, it appears did not want to do so, was likely not given a choice.

PART IV

CHAPTER 52

JOURNEYING ON WITH THE CHURCH

Having traveled many spiritual miles since the Chamblee Road experience, one thing remains clear: the stories in the Bible that touched me as a child are still important to me. The Exodus story was the first to capture my imagination. As a little girl I had no way of knowing how deeply it had become imbedded in my heart and mind. I was on a journey, as I believe we all are, and God calls us forth to new life amidst the trials along the way. In that sense we are like the ancient Hebrews traveling toward the Promised Land, part of a rag tag army making our way to a place called home. The church played a vital part as my traveling companion and to this day inspires and motivates me as I dig deeper into its history and theology. In my case I speak of the United Methodist Church, which I have served as both lay person and clergy.

Mystics and reformers in church history became my heroes and heroines, some of whom lost their lives due to the challenges they posed for the institution as well as the culture of their day. I wished for their courage. People like Francis who was named a saint, Meister Eckert, Hildegard of Bingen, Julian of Norwich, John Wesley, Sojourner Truth and Martin Luther King Jr. to name a few.

The church needed to be challenged throughout history just as it does in our time. There came a time when I could no longer repeat some of the creeds used in Sunday morning services without doing the research I had also been doing with scripture. What was going on in the church when they were written, what did they mean to us as twenty-first Century Christians?

The church has been the keeper of scripture over the centuries. The ways in which it has been interpreted has been both blessing and curse to the world. Errors in translations from the ancient languages into modern vernacular were inevitable. Monks and scholars who hand copied the Bible in the early Christian era faced a daunting task without the benefit of archeological information unearthed in the last century. Greater understanding of the ancient texts we are privileged to have today allows for new insight and meaning as well.

For many of us who believed as children that God reached out of the clouds and with His/Her own hand wrote the sacred words, it became quite an adventure to learn who wrote the various documents, their reasons for doing so, for whom the words were written and when the various writings came into being. This naturally led to the larger question as to the authority of the Bible. By looking at the context in which scripture was written, people were heard questioning what some passages had to do with our lives today. The response heard to such an inspection of scripture would sound something like, *Wait, are you saying the Bible isn't true? Is it not inspired by God and thus holy? You can't just throw out what you think isn't important. Where would this lead?* A humorous statement made in the 1960s at our church in Miami, Florida comes to mind, "If the King James Version was good enough for Jesus, it's good enough for me." Many Christians, including myself, however, were led to examine the theology we had heard and digested at an earlier stage of life and, as we did, begin to seriously grapple with concepts in the Bible. Undergraduate school along with a degree in theology gave me ample opportunity to do this.

At the little house church I attended with Mrs. Smith (Chapter 15, *The Devil, Pot Roast, and Handel*) I heard about Adam and Eve. Of course, we wouldn't expect its telling to include historic data when taught to children. It would be years before I learned it was one of two creation stories, the first story expressing in poetic form a creation that took place in six days with God resting on the seventh with all of creation, including humankind, men and women declared good: Two very different stories, written by different authors at different periods of Israel's history, for different reasons. Am I saying the authors were not inspired by God? Of course they were. Am I saying they were not meant to be taken literally? Yes, I am.

What I learned at the little church at the end of a gravel road was that Adam and Eve disobeyed God and were sent out of a beautiful garden where God had come to visit them every evening. What made the news even worse for a little girl was that it was Eve's fault. She was tempted by the talking snake and ate from the forbidden tree. The man and woman had disobeyed God and Eve was to blame, according to early Christian writings, an example of the misuse of scripture. The doctrine of original sin was planted in my mind, and my heart was the worst for it. I had joined the ranks of believers in the Western World.

The Bishop of Hippo, Augustine, is recognized to be the author of the doctrine. Born in Algeria in 354 CE and said to be the Father of Western Theology, he wrote extensively about the matter of sin and its resulting effect on humankind. According to him we are all born in sin making us at odds with God and thus unable to relate to Him. This wrote Augustine, was the condition into which infants were born, making them sinners from the beginning who needed Christ. Since Jesus took on the likeness of sinful flesh in order to renew it, without infant baptism babies who died without the ritual were unable to enter the kingdom of God. What were we to do? Of course, baptize infants and when old enough to understand the need for Christ they could accept Jesus as the Savior who was sent to die for their sins.

Original sin was the reason God sent Jesus to die, not just to renew but to save us. Something about that really confused me when I first heard it, thinking of a father that would do this to a child. Yet, since I didn't know how to make myself better I thought it was a good thing that Jesus did this for me.

It would be many years before I came to see the harmful effects this teaching had on me as it fostered an understanding of a distant God who was to be feared and who had needed a sacrifice because of my sinful nature. Even though I heard that Jesus died for my sins—the message from most of the churches I attended as a child—I still didn't have the assurance of being good enough to merit God's acceptance.

Despite the negative theology I continued to grab hold of the stories in both the Old and New Testaments. I did not, however, realize the stories I loved were taking hold of me in a deep place within, giving me direction for my life and creating ways of handling life's challenges.

CHAPTER 53

WHAT WE DO WITH THE BIBLE

"The B-i-b-l-e, the only book for me. I stand alone on the Word of God, the B-i-b-l-e." I sang this song in the Sunday schools I attended as a child and my children sang it as well. The Bible is primary to the lives of both Christians and Jews. I cannot count the number of times I have been troubled, grieving, in physical pain, or unable to sleep and have turned to the Bible, opened it at random and found just what I needed. It's not an act of magic. There is so much in the Bible to help us that we are bound to open to what we need at any given moment. I like to think it is the power of the Spirit that is answering our prayers for help. John Wesley, the founder of Methodism, made this a habit throughout his life and urged others to do the same. Then, of course, as we become familiar with passages that bring comfort or strength we can turn to them when the need arises.

How often I have opened to Psalm 23 and thought of the Christ as the Good Shepherd who leads me to a safe place of rest expressed in verse two, "In grassy meadows he lets me lie," and "By tranquil streams he leads me to restore my spirit." When struggling with a sense of failure or having made poor choices, Psalm 51 has expressed what I thought and felt. The words King David spoke to the prophet Nathan after being confronted by him for his sin against God have been my own plea. "Have mercy on me, O God, in your faithful love. In your great tenderness wipe away my offences." Our situations may be very different from David's and yet we know the pain of choices that have hurt others and had negative results for ourselves.

When going through loss and grief, Romans 8:18-20 has brought me through difficult days. I thank Paul for writing in his letter, "In my estimation, all that we suffer in the present time is nothing in comparison with the glory which is destined to be disclosed for us, for the whole creation is waiting with eagerness for the children of God to be revealed." In many passages Jesus is recorded to have spoken words of hope and healing to those in need. There is no doubt the Bible offers inspiration for all circumstances of life. But what of taking passages out of context to justify our already held beliefs? I think now of the hard sayings that are found in both the Old and New Testaments.

We human beings can find just about anything we want in the Bible to uphold our already established beliefs. Once a passage is found it can be used to argue our case, emotionally hit another over the head, so to speak, or write them off as unworthy of God's love since he or she is not obeying scripture. What the Bible says and how we interpret what it says is vital to how we express our Christian faith.

The term "proof text" is just what it says, to prove something based on a text. Thankfully I have never heard anyone quote a passage from Deuteronomy I discovered as a young adult making my way through the Old Testament. I planned to read the Bible from beginning to end but ran out of steam before accomplishing it. Coming upon some passages proved too perplexing to me. The verses in Deuteronomy 21:18-23 for instance, gives instructions as to how to deal with a willful and disobedient son. It reads: "If a man has a stubborn and rebellious son who will not listen to the voice either of his father or of his mother and, even when they punish him, still will not pay attention to them, his father and mother must take hold of him and bring him out to the elders of his town at the gate of that place. To the elders of his town, they will say, 'This son of ours is stubborn and rebellious and will not listen to us, he is a wastrel and a drunkard.' All his fellow-citizens must then stone him to death."

I once spoke with a Torah scholar about this passage. What did her congregation do with such an admonition? Her answer, "This, and other hard sayings, were not merely overlooked or considered to be irrelevant. Rather the rabbis of her Reform Synagogue go through the entire Torah (Genesis, Exodus, Leviticus, Deuteronomy and Numbers) each year to determine how the laws recorded in them speak to the age in which we live." Their conclusion regarding the disobedient son stunned me and gave me a good laugh. It was, "There never was such a son and there never were such parents." The scholar went on to say if there was, the family would be placed in the care of the whole congregation that would offer their support and practical help in dealing with the son. I absolutely loved this interpretation and thought about the way other communities of faith deal with the passages that seem untenable.

There are many more hard sayings in scripture, most we shudder at the thought of embracing. For instance, women are included in lists of property along with cattle and land in the book of Deuteronomy and justification for slavery supported by some Christians is based on the story of Noah and his son Ham in Genesis 9:18-29. I once read a sermon preached prior to the Civil War that informed some congregation in the south that they would be going against the will of God to free the slaves based on this passage. God was believed to have sanctioned slavery for African descendants.

Thankfully I have never heard a sermon based on the above verses but I do see practical help within congregations through uplifting worship, prayer and Bible study groups, grief recovery groups and pastoral counseling. And not to overlook fellowship based on a shared faith. These seem closely akin to what my friend in the Jewish community was describing as their response to a family in difficulty. Being in a supportive community can be a powerful tool for all events of life. It has been for me and my family.

The tendency is to overlook the verses we would find impossible to keep like the one advising the stoning of a child and moving to the ones that condemn who or what we think should be condemned, case in point, homosexuals and lesbians or LGBT (Lesbian, Gay, Bisexual, Transsexual, a more inclusive term). I have thought on occasion that Momma may have been in a lesbian relationship with Joyce Reynolds who is mentioned in the chapter, The Spa Hotel. It may be the case though my sense is that Momma's loneliness and need of affection led her to people who would fill that need regardless of their sexual orientation.

CHAPTER 54

A POINT OF CONTENTION

The issue of sexuality and gender identity is one of the major divisions among Christians in our day. My early experience in church was to never hear it mentioned. In fact, sexuality in general was never mentioned. I occasionally heard derogatory terms to describe some people and as a teenager turned to the dictionary for definitions. What was a fag? What did the word sodomy mean? The time had come to educate myself. I turned to the public library as I had done so many times in the past.

In the 1980s a women's clergy retreat was held at the Glorietta Conference Center outside Albuquerque, New Mexico. We had worship every day and one service was planned and conducted by a group of lesbian clergywomen. *OK, I'm alright with this* I thought. Little did I know it would shake my foundation and force me to examine my thoughts and feelings about my homosexual colleagues? I had no doubt that I was a heterosexual human but how did I feel about these women who had openly declared they were not? Then I wondered about how it was for them? Were they nervous or feeling scared? They were, after all, announcing to all in attendance, "We're different, we are different." I thought they were brave and they might also have felt proud to be standing together and owning who they were.

My reaction to the turmoil this stirred up in me was that I got sick. I left the conference with fever, sore throat, aches and pains.

Once home I began to search for references in the Bible. Then I pulled out the research tools used in seminary and reviewed who wrote the passages, when were they written, who they were written for, and what they say to us today? I found few direct citations on the subject. The first being the story of Sodom and Gomorrah (Genesis 19) and the last a statement attributed to Paul in a letter in I Timothy 1: 9-10, a letter that many scholars do not believe was written by Paul.

The story of Sodom and Gomorrah has been interpreted over the centuries to represent the homosexual sin that existed in these two cities and thus God's reason for destroying them. Many scholars question aspects of this passage. That these two were "sin cities" is not called into doubt but the actual nature of the sin is. The two visitors who came to Lot's home were called angels, the same ones who had visited Abram and Sarai and told them they would become parents of a son even though they were up in years. Angels were seen as God's messengers bringing information from God, thus all sojourners or strangers were to be welcomed and even honored. One might very well be such a messenger. The demand of the mob in Sodom was to bring the strangers out to them so they "could know them" and Lot refused, offering his two daughters in their place. Since there was no understanding of homosexuality as it might be seen in two people of the same sex in a committed relationship, the passage is seen for what it is, namely about violence against the two strangers. It was about rape and is condemned as it should be in any age.

To reiterate, there is no term defining homosexuality in scripture just as there is no reference to people of the same gender in a loving and committed relationship. Purity laws do reject same-sex-relations. Yahweh had given the law to create a distinctive people different from those who inhabited the land they were entering. Cults already in existence proved seductive to the people of Israel and were seen as a threat to their future. The people were called back from idolatrous worship again and again, especially from the cult of Baal.

In II Kings 23:7, a reform movement records the destruction of the homes of male prostitutes who participated in the worship of Baal. To succumb to the lure of Baalism would break the first commandment to love Yahweh alone. There was a practical reason for avoiding same-sex activity as well. Such unions did not produce off springs which were vital to the growing nation of Israel. Under no circumstances were the Hebrews to participate in the religions of the land. Same partner sex approved by foreign cults may well have been a factor in the strong warnings against it in Old Testament law.

Procreation was not the only reason for marriage, but it was an important one. Since the Hebrews did not have a clear doctrine of immortality at that time sons were vital in perpetuating one's lineage. Sons preserved the father's name and personality and were important to the entire clan.

Along with same-sex relationships the purity laws in Deuteronomy and Leviticus list other conditions under which people were deemed unclean and not allowed to worship with the community. These included women who had given birth, menstruating women, those who were blind, identified as lame, dwarfed, or had touched or eaten pork. We wouldn't think of calling such people unclean and, thus, unable to participate in worship today, though some do this through the condemnation of gays and lesbians.

As many before me have pointed out, Jesus voiced no such judgment against homosexuality or lesbian people. Paul did, however.

Paul was a Pharisaic Jew, trained under the famous rabbi and teacher, Gamaliel. Before his Damascus Road experience he was zealous in keeping the Law given to Moses. Readers of the Book of Acts see his growing hostility toward the new followers of Jesus as he went about the country and into Syria to arrest those who were to him, infidels.

After his experience on the Damascus Road his life changed course and he began to preach to the Gentiles as well as Jews and to establish churches. He, like his ancestors before him, faced the challenge of establishing new communities in a world dominated by the worship of other gods, now the deities of Greece and Rome. He clearly spelled out his position on sexual behavior in I Corinthians as well as in other of his letters. He did not want the new Christians to be mistaken for those who were following the ways of the world and he does include sodomites in his list of evil-doers who will never inherit the Kingdom of God. Christians were being called on to refuse the standards of the world and to allow nothing to get in the way of their allegiance to Christ.

In that day there was no understanding that a person could be born a homosexual or lesbian and many today still believe that such attraction is purely choice. I can no more throw out the science regarding our gender than I could dismiss the science of creation. I am convinced after hearing the stories of many and looking at what science has to say on the subject that gender identity is not a choice. Often those who finally accept the fact that they are "different," including a dear grandson of mine, have struggled for years in an attempt to deny their homosexual or lesbian nature.

Paul did not have such information, but did know of immorality that hurt the parties involved and thus should be denounced. Indiscriminate sexual behavior, whether heterosexual or homosexual, hurts us as human beings. I believe Paul was writing about promiscuous, predatory, or non-consensual same sex acts between people whom he understood as being heterosexual.

Paul's understanding of the Christ in whom there is "neither Jew nor Greek, there can be neither slave nor freeman, there can be neither male nor female, for you are all one in Christ Jesus," Galatians 3:28 was leading people to a higher spiritual understanding. His story is a great adventure of faith and of change. One who upheld the letter of the Law of Moses reached a point in his relationship with Christ that led to a sharp turn surprising his Jewish colleagues and pointing to the change of thought taking place in him. He declared the new gentile converts to the Jesus movement did not have to follow the Law that required male circumcision, an unquestioned requirement of his Hebrew tradition.

After exploring scripture on the subject of gender differences I had the opportunity to attend a seminar on the subject at a counseling center where I was studying.

CHAPTER 55

A FIRST-HAND ACCOUNT

Frank had been in seminary when I was there. After graduation and ordination he moved to another part of the country, continued his education, and became a Pastoral Counselor. This was partly due to the United Methodist position on homosexuality which states, "The practice of homosexuality is incompatible with Christian teaching. Therefore self-avowed practicing homosexuals are not to be certified as candidates, ordained as ministers; or appointed to serve in The United Methodist Church." (Article 304.3 of The 2012 Book of Discipline) He had been asked to talk to our group when he came back to Dallas for a visit.

Frank was a kind man, quiet but yet quick to greet people and to enter into conversation with them. I liked him. Some years before I heard he had experienced a nervous breakdown, as debilitating depressive episodes were then called. He had been hospitalized. On this day he stood before a group of therapists, counselors, and ministers to tell us his story and provide us with information on the subject of homosexuality.

He spoke of knowing he was different while still a teen and of the inner turmoil he endured during those years. At first he tried denying the feelings and thoughts that he might be gay. He didn't want to be. He wanted a family someday. He wanted children. Not thinking he could talk to his own family or friends he continued to keep secret what was becoming more and more obvious to him. Frank then spoke about the depression that finally overwhelmed him.

I felt empathy for him as I received information that added to my understanding of sexual preference. First of all, it was not a choice, but rather something one is born with. While many people refute this, even as they deny other research findings from science, one point was particularly credible in my mind. As in the world of humans, same-sex attraction is seen in the animal world. I could affirm that. We have had pets that exhibited it. Why would we condemn someone for something that was a part of their human make-up?

Frank talked to us about criticism aimed particularly at gay men. They took part in outlandish gay parades, often acted inappropriately in public, engaged in sex for sex sake alone. With exception of the parades we could say the same thing about numbers of heterosexual men. Gays often have few role models to emulate and little if any dating experience in their teen years. Add to this the fact that there is often condemnation from family and friends as well as being ostracized from the religious communities in which they grew up. Their experience has been different from those of heterosexual persons.

Finally, we don't usually hear of gay and lesbian people who are living their lives, working, being students and doing the same things we all do but without the right in most places to make their relationship legal.

I was impressed with Frank's courage to speak the truth about himself and for persevering through his painful experiences. I could take to heart Jesus admonition not to judge that I not be judged in like manner.

CHAPTER 56

A PLACE AT THE TABLE

I continue to be grateful for the stories in the Bible that spoke to me as a child. I grabbed hold of the Exodus story as a little girl without recognizing just how important it would become over the years. Looking back I can see it was a call to leave the slavery of depression and make my way through a sort of wilderness that seemed to me as much a journey as the one undertaken by the early Hebrews. Uncertainty and fear stalked me at times from thoughts I had absorbed of an angry and punishing God but these did not overthrow my sense of God's goodness. There were many stories in scripture to uphold what I experienced of God through nature and through the many people who helped me during difficult times. Luke's Gospel, Chapter 14:15-24 records another treasured story, this one attributed to Jesus.

There is no telling when I first heard this story of the

Great Banquet. It has long spoken to me about God's inclusive love for all creation including those I think of as the "little people," those on the margins of society like my mother. I also believe the story is a fine example of Jesus's sense of humor. When making this statement to an adult Sunday School Class I was teaching many years ago, it became clear that one man in attendance was not happy. He didn't bother to raise his hand but brusquely asked his question.

"Little lady, just where did you get such ideas."

It was my first time to teach an adult class at my home church and the man's demeanor and the pointedness of his question was a bit unnerving. Nevertheless, without flinching, realizing he had a problem with Jesus being so human as to have a sense of humor, I asked him a question in return.

"Sir, will you hear me out? At the end of this class we can talk more about it if you'd like." *Ok*, I thought, *now keep going*. He crossed his arms, resting them on top of a mid-section that extended beyond the rest of his body, then sat back with a look that was far from friendly. I opened my Bible and read from chapter 14 where Jesus is sitting in the home of a leading Pharisee as a guest for a Sabbath meal. There are numbers of passages that find him at table sharing a meal. Doing so in that day was an act full of meaning, a way of saying *we are one*, we can trust each other. The story opens with a discussion about the seating arrangement. The next segment is the one I most cherish.

The food was prepared and the banquet made ready when the householder sent servants out to invite people to attend. One can readily see this approach was very different than what we do in our time when notes asking "would be" attendees to, *keep this date open* are sent out weeks ahead followed by the invitation closer to the day of the event. It had to be so. There was no refrigeration in order to prepare foods ahead so when the word went out those who were invited gladly responded with their presence. In this case, however, people gave reasons for not doing so and, I think would have evoked laughter on the part of the listeners.

The first one, "I can't come. I bought a piece of land and must go see it." Purchasing land was a big deal and no one would buy a plot or acreage without seeing it, walking it, and approving of its possible productivity before buying it. Poor excuse.

The second invitee said he couldn't come to the banquet because he just bought five, mind you, *five,* yoke of oxen. This reason must have brought a good belly laugh. The poorest of the poor would not be able to afford one yoke of oxen in Jesus's time and those who could would have tried them out to see how they performed the work of plowing *before* making them their own. Another poor excuse.

The third reason for not coming to the banquet was due to conjugal responsibilities since a man had just married. People in that day were very different than in our own time. This would have been equivalent to saying; *you know how it is when you're first married.* This would not have happened.

You know where the story goes. The householder sends his servants to the edge of town into the streets and alleys, some versions call it the hedgerows or just beyond the city limits. They deliver the invitation to all who are there—the lame, blind, poor and oppressed people. At first these folks refused the invitation, too. This was expected, and a common practice in Jesus's day. When being invited by someone above their station in life one would be expected to refuse, saying he or she was not worthy of such an honor. After several such refusals the person would relent and accept. Some translations used the word *compel* to describe the manner in which the marginal people were invited. Sad to say this was translated as forcing them and used in the Inquisition centuries later to require Jews to renounce Judaism and join the Catholic Church.

So who was invited to the banquet? Everyone!

In this story Momma was invited, so was Tony, along with my upright teachers and neighbors, along with all those community helpers, and even me. We were all invited. Needless to say I loved this story. It remains one of my favorites to this day. We all have a place at the table and I am grateful beyond words.

The man who asked where I got this idea did not wish to discuss it further. *Had he realized, he too had been invited to the table?*

CHAPTER 57

A TABLE CONVERSATION

The Bible with its wide range of writings has remained a source of inspiration and the subject of my research for many decades. My struggle to better understand its meaning continues, though the questions about heaven and hell that troubled me with regard to my mother are no longer worrisome. While there are certainly consequences to the choices we make in life, I am convinced that some persons have far fewer choices than others. Momma's handicaps left her with few options.

The answer I received after her death opened the way for this understanding. God is merciful just as Jesus demonstrated God to be. Hell is a sense of being separated from God, from others, and from our true selves. I have been in hell on several occasions in my long life. To me heaven is reunion, a right relationship in which trust and commitment exist. It can be experienced right here, right now, with God, one another, and within ourselves. I believe the process of growing in our relationship with our Creator continues beyond this earthly life and that Momma is moving along nicely.

My theology began in simplicity, taking in the stories and, without knowing it, making them my own. It moved to complexity in looking beyond the literal to the symbolic enabling me to better understand their meaning. From there I have returned to simplicity. God loves us and wants to be in relationship with us.

From beginning to end the Bible tells me that God is Creator, calling forth all that is and declaring it to be good. That goodness includes all of us since we are spiritual and created in God's own image, which is Spirit. The Hebrews were given the Law, not by an arbitrary God but from Love itself, providing guidelines for living harmoniously. I believe we have been evolving spiritually and are still on our way to becoming fully human. We are living in the awareness that God is immanent, dwelling within each one of us, as well as transcendent, filling all space.

Jesus, more than any person, was in complete union with His Father/Mother God. This is a statement of faith on my part. His message was not accepted by the powers of the world in his day and is still rejected both by conscious choice and through misinterpretation of his message of love, mercy, and justice. He taught and lived with compassion, action-based yearning for justice, and trust in God. He lives even now. For these reasons I call

Him Lord and Savior.

I believe Momma would have loved Him if someone had told her.

FORGIVENESS & GRATITUDE

As a result of writing this memoir, initially intended for my children and grandchildren, I became aware of forgiveness for my family as well as a tremendous sense of gratitude for the many individuals and organizations that contributed to my growing up. The recognition came that my family of origin did the best they could under the circumstances of their lives. I came to see they would have done a better job in caring for me had they had the inner resources and motivation to do so. Lingering sadness and the fear of debilitating depression that would require hospitalization disappeared with this awareness.

Tony was a person not geared to succeed in life. He didn't seem concerned about regular employment, having a home or being a respected member of the community. Even so, he taught me so much in an odd sort of way. Observing his manner of "making things work for him," I decided to live my life in the opposite fashion. To this day I pay my bills on time and cherish my home. He taught me "what not to do."

Emma and Grandpa had their own burdens, most from the past but challenges in the present as well. Though not written of in depth in *A Place at the Table*, they both experienced much sadness in their lives. In my family research I learned they lost three children who died in infancy due to childhood diseases. They both provided a model for hard work, persistence during times of trial, and evidence of joy that came through music and keeping the memories of their homeland alive. I loved them both and am grateful I could go to their home when there was little money coming in. For a child who moved more times than I can remember, the model of a family living in one house became the picture of home I held dear and promised myself to duplicate one day.

My primary caregiver, Momma, did not have the ability to do any better and, unlike my own experience as an adult, did not know how to find help with regard to child-rearing. Momma, I forgive you and hold you dear in my heart today.

Dreams have been important messengers to me just as they were for many in ancient times as recorded in scripture. I clearly remember one I had a number of years ago that gave me reassurance of my mother's ongoing journey.

The setting of the dream was an ice cream parlor and candy shop I had been in a number of times. In the front of the shop just inside the door was a small round table covered with a lace table cloth. Light was pouring in from the large window next to it. Momma sat in a chair across from where I was sitting. We were eating ice cream from crystal dishes and enjoying the rich tastes. Momma looked healthy and serene. We ate in silence just enjoying each other's presence.

I believe the dream was a sign of Momma's current condition, call it heaven or another state of reality. It is about me as well. My mind is not capable of a clear explanation. I can only say thank you, God. We all have a place at the table. When we receive the invitation to the banquet, let's accept.

ACKNOWLEDGMENTS

I'd like to thank my family—husband Doug, daughter Lynda, son Russell, and daughter Amy who left us in body but remains forever in our hearts. Our children and their beloved spouses have given us seven grandchildren. Three great-grandchildren and a partner to a grandson have joined our ranks as well. Together we make up the family I longed for as a child. I love them all very much.

My deep thanks to the members of my Writer's Group that encouraged me to keep writing. It was within the safe confines of our circle that I began to share the memories of growing up.

My special thanks to Kathy Kuenzer, a fellow writer and friend who was instrumental in my appointment to a United Methodist Church in Plano, Texas and then became a coach as I began writing. Thanks too, to Carole Deily, writer, librarian, and friend of long standing. I don't think I would have completed this book without the support of these two women.

My gratitude goes to Tina Ferguson, author, business woman, artist, and intuitive visionary. I have been blessed by her persistent encouragement and practical help in completing and publishing *A Place at the Table*.

Finally I thank my dear daughter Lynda DeGrow Kingsley for her painting on the book cover that captures the essence of my story. She is a talented woman who has inspired me in so many ways.

ABOUT THE AUTHOR

Katherine DeGrow lives in Richardson, Texas with her husband Doug. A former United Methodist Minister and Pastoral Counselor, she is the mother of three children, and also is grandmother to seven grandchildren and three great-grandchildren.

37001707R00182

Made in the USA
Charleston, SC
22 December 2014